Rio For Partiers

WHAT TO DO WHEN A CARIOCA SAYS

NETWORK SELECTION:

| PHONE SETTINGS | MANUAL NETWORK SELECTION | TIM BRASIL OR 724 02 BRA 02 |

MENU   SEARCH

MULTILINGUAL CUSTOMER CARE. JUST DIAL ***144** FROM YOUR GSM PHONE OR **0800 741 4141** FROM ANY PHONE.

* To check handset compatibility and further coverage information, access www.tim.com.br

TALK TO YOU AROUND".

The Cariocas, the folks from Rio, are a receptive and welcoming people, and so, one of their habits is to always say good-bye with **"talk to you around"**, or **"call me up"**. At this moment, a tourist without a phone may be completely lost. What to do? Bring your GSM set and choose TIM as your mobile phone operator in Brazil. So, in addition to phoning, you can send to your friends back home SMS messages, photos and videos of your trip or even access the internet.*

Choose TIM and relax, because in a little while you're going to look like a local.

SELECT THE ONLY OPERATOR WITH
GSM COVERAGE ALL OVER BRAZIL.*

TIM

Viver sem fronteiras

Rio For Partiers

2007 © Copyright Editora Solcat Ltda,
First Published 2003 - All rights reserved
- Editora Solcat Ltda.

Photography: João Penoni e Cristiano Nogueira, Ricardo Zerrener, RioTur, Agencia Globo et al.

No part of this publication may be reproduced, stored in a retrieval system or transmitted in any form or by any means electronic, mechanical or otherwise, without permission of the copyright holder.
The products, trademarks, logos and proprietary shapes used in this book are copyrighted or otherwise protected by legislation and can not be reproduced without the permission of the holder of the rights.

ISBN 85-89992-01-2

The editors of the book did their best to offer information that was up to date at the time of printing. However, some data is subject to change and the editors cannot accept responsibility for changes that have occurred since the book's printing.

Readers interested in sending their suggestions, ideas or complaints can do so via email at cris@rioforpartiers.com or by writing to our postal address:

Solcat Editora
Rua Visconde de Pirajá 48 SL 702, Ipanema, Rio de Janeiro, RJ CEP 22411-000 Brazil
tel:21-2523-9857 USA: 1-312 238-8998
web: www.rioforpartiers.com

Part of "For Partiers" series of guides. Published and printed in Brazil by Editora Solcat Ltda.
Sixth Edition.

Nogueira, Cristiano
Rio For Partiers / by Cristiano Nogueira ; [photography João Penoni and author]. -- Rio de Janeiro :
Solcat Editora, 2007. -- (For partiers)

1. Rio de Janeiro (RJ) - Descrição e viagens - Guias
I. Penoni, João. II. Título. II. Série

03-5742   CDD-918.153

The SolCat Team

Cristiano Nogueira
Editor, writer and art director

Priscilla Tipping
Marketing

Veronica Isbarrola
Distribution

Gustavo Trompowsky
Partnership coordinator

Ronaldo Alperin
Researcher

Felipe Moraes
Illustrator and graphic designer

Derwl-Derwl
Company dog and chief order barker

MISSING:

Marina Macacchero- Map designer, João Penoni-Photographer.
Luis F. Nunes - research assistant, Pauline Harris - proof reader

CONTRIBUTING WRITERS

Phil Smith: Business in Brazil & Brazilian Pride; Dan Littauner: Gay Rio; India Lee Borba: How to Deal with Brazilian Boys

PHOTO CREDITS

João Penoni, Cristiano Nogueira, Dan Littauner, Agência Globo Ricardo Zerrenner (RZ) (www.zerrenner.fot.br), Biblioteca Nacional, Riotur, Iko Olivier (IK): opetit@gmail.com Ernani Bezerra(ER), Sam Stearman (SS): Sam's Exotic Travel Photos - www.samsays.com, David Rice (DR), Amy Sastro (AS), Preston Grant (PG): www.prestongrant.com; sports instructors and Secretarias de Turismo of their respective states.

Rio For

Partiers

by Cristiano Nogueira

Check our site for updates
www.rioforpartiers.com

CONTENTS

How to Use this Guide
(You've got to read this first)

To tell you exactly what the best activities to do during each day of your stay in Rio, we split up the Guide into 3 sections:

1) the Daytime Guide

2) the Nighttime Guide.

3) the Dinner Guide

This way, you can choose whatever you are in the mood for during the day and align your dinner and nighttime activity to your appetite and night of the week.

Daytime Activities

The day time Guide will assume you will be waking up at around 10 or 11am, getting a late breakfast at one of the juice bars, then doing one of the following activities:

Relaxing: activities which do not involve too much physical or mental effort.

Sport: activities which involve physical activity.

Cultural: tours which involve reading, learning and other mental activities.

Rainy day: indoor activities you might as well consider.

Nighttime activities

Nighttime suggestions are ordered according to the night of the week since some places are better on some days than others. At the same time, for each day of the week, you have 4 different types of nightlife: clubbing, street party, live music and relaxing.

After the nighttime suggestions, be sure to stop at one of the after-hours food spots to soothe your stomach.

Food Guide

There are 12 dinner and 4 lunch suggestions, which cover the different styles of Brazilian cuisine. There are expensive, average and inexpensive recommendations. We then explain all the street snacks, drinks, bar foods and desserts you will encounter.

Carioca= a native of Rio

Ipanema beach, Two Brothers mountain in background

RIO STATS AND KEYS

TELEPHONES:

How to Call

Rio de Janeiro to USA: 00 31 + country code (i.e.: 1 for USA) + area code + telephone number

To call from Rio De Janeiro to other cities in Brazil=

0 + 31 + city area code + telephone number

ARRIVING IN RIO

Distance between International Airport Antônio Carlos Jobim (GIG) to Copacabana = 20 Km (30min) = roughly R$40

Distance between Santos Dumont Airport to Copa= 15 Km = roughly R$20

Bus station: Rodoviária Novo Rio Tel: 2263-5828 Ext. 192 Distance Copa to Novo Rio =20km = R$20

CLIMATE

Rio De Janeiro is a subtropical city.

Summer December to March with temperatures 25°C (77°F) to 42°C (108°F);

Winter June to August, temperature around 20°C (68°F) to 16°C (60°F).

ELECTRIC SOCKET

Electric voltage: 110V. (some hotels have 220V. adaptors)

SHOPPING

Tip: 10% of the total : usually already included

Commerce hours: 9pm. to 7pm

Shopping centers: 10am to 10pm

Banks: 10am to 4 pm

Cash machines: from 6am to 10pm

Cash machines At Galeão/ Santos Dumont/ Rodoviária are 24h.

SUBWAY STATION

From monday to saturday: from 5am to 12am

Sunday and holidays from 7am to 11pm.

RIO DE JANEIRO'S NEIGHBORING STATES

West: Minas Gerais

North: Espírito Santo

Southwest: São Paulo

East: Atlantic Ocean

PUBLIC HOLIDAYS

1st of January : New Years

20th of January - Saint Sebastian : Only In Rio

Shifting dates in Feb - Carnival

Shifting in Mar - Holy Week

21st of April - Tiradentes (Independence hero)

23 of April - Saint George (Only In Rio)

1st of May - Labor Day

Shifting dates in June - Corpus Christi

7 of September - Independence Day

12 of October - Our Lady of Apparition - Brazil's Holy Lady

2nd of November - Finados

15th of November - Republic Proclamation

20th of November - Zumbi Dos Palmares : Black Consciousness

25th of December - Christmas

Botafogo bay with Sugar Loaf Mountain, Niterói city in the background

BRAZILIAN

PEOPLE

1. Pelé (the best soccer player ever: these days he promotes more brands than Proctor & Gamble)

2. Gisele Bundchen (tall, beautiful, magical legs, supermodel)

3. Hans Stern (possibly the world's most influential jeweler::H.Stern)

4. Lula (NOT the female singer who was big in the sixties: HE is the President!)

5. Ronaldo (number 9: bald, big teeth, incredibly skilled soccer star)

6. Ronaldinho (number 10: dreads, big teeth, incredibly skilled soccer star)

7. Gilberto Gil (singer, song writer, actor, politician: dreads, aging rock star)

8. Fernando Meirelles (film director of "Cidade de Deus" about gangs in Rio favelas)

9. Ayrton Senna (Formula One driver: RIP)

10. Nelson Piquet (Formula One driver: still going)

11. Zico (another soccer star, now a top-notch coach)

12. Carmen Miranda (1940s actress, beautiful, born in Portugal, adopted by Brazilians)

13. Chico Mendes (Amazon rainforest activist, murdered in 1988)

14. Roberto Marinho (founding father of O Globo media empire, recently died at age 98)

15. Xuxa (Former wife of Pelé: TV presenter, singer, THE QUEEN OF THE KIDS)

16. Chico Buarque (singer/poet/composer/genius)

17. Jorge Amado (one of Brazil's most popular writers: Go to Bahia to check out a UNESCO-listed house, constructed in his honor)

18. Jose and Antonio Ermino de Moraes (richest men in Brazil, brothers)

FACTS

1. Brazil has 20% of the world's fresh water supply (China has 20% of the world's people!)

2. There are 184 million of them! (July 2004, so even more now!)

3. They all speak the same language! (Portuguese)

4. You can not tell a Brazilian by simply looking at them (we have the most diverse mix of races and cultures in the world)

5. Two thirds of them live near the coast (or should we say "By the beach!")

6. Caipirinhas are possibly the best drink in the world to sip at sunset.

7. Every year they host the biggest parties in the world: Carnival!! Come and join us in February every year! (Or New Year's Eve for the World's second biggest party!)

8. They produce over 50% of the world's coffee!

PRIDE by Phil Smith

9. Iguaçu Falls, in the southern state of Paraná, is bigger than both Niagara and Victoria Falls! (60 feet higher than Niagara and about one and a half times as wide)

10. As well as beach football, we play Fresco ball, which is like tennis, only we don't let the ball bounce.

11. Brazil has the highest number of species of primates, amphibians and plants in the world, and is in the top five in the world for numbers of birds and reptile species. A typical acre of Amazonian rainforest will support around 250 species of tree, compared with around 10 species an acre in typical forests in Europe.

12. As well as being expert dancers in samba, zouk, pagode, chorinho, bossa nova and forró, Brazil is also home to capoeira, a unique blend of dancing, martial arts and traditional music.

Odd

Favelas (slums) have the highest percentage world-wide of civil engineers (all unlicensed).

Posto 9 and 10 (Ipanema) and Praia do Pepe have the highest ratio of sculptured bodies.

Quotes

Fifteen reasons why Brazilians are proud to be "Brazilian"

(Real quotes from Real Brazilians on Ipanema beach!)

1. "Because of the unique energy of the Brazilian people."

2. "Brazil is a happy and passionate nation"

3. "We have the best natural resources and natural beauty in the world"

4. "We are always optimistic!"

5. "Because of all the beautiful women!"

6. "We are very hospitable, spiritual and sensual."

7. "We are very open and fun."

8. "We are simple, not complicated, happy, and very friendly"

9. "Because of the solidarity here. We are very hospitable, communicative and our people have a wonderful temperament."

10. "We have the best football team in the world."

11. "We live well and enjoy the natural beauty that God has given us"

12. "We have incredible cultural diversity which gives us strength and a feeling of togetherness."

13. "We love our music!"

14. "The truth is that the combination of the people and natural beauty makes Brazil a unique and happy place."

15. "We are Party People!" (Festeiros)

But Most of All...

Happiest people in the world! According to two independent sociological studies in US and German universities. After analyzing in different countries various factors such as emotional balance, financial stability, nutrition, health, family, love, sex, stress and professional outlook, Brazil came out on top of both studies. Nigeria in 2nd place. They concluded that the happiest countries were the ones where its citizens' perception of and hope for life improvement are high. Dealing a blow to political theories, 2 Scandinavian countries came out close to the bottom.

Rio is split up into 4 zones: the South Zone, the North Zone, the West Zone and the downtown area (Centro). As far as general tourism is concerned, the only zone of interest is the South and the downtown area.

North Zone

The North Zone is mostly poor neighborhoods, with very little appeal to tourists. With the exception of the Tijuca Forest, Maracana and the Salgueiro samba school rehearsals, no other visits are necessary.

West Zone

The West Zone includes everything after Barra da Tijuca (commonly referred to as Barra). Barra is a new middle-upper class neighborhood with tons of shopping areas and night-life. It is, however, mostly modelled on the average American suburb, with large avenues, strip malls and ample parking. Unless you have never seen an American suburb in your life, we recommend limiting your visits here to Pepe Beach, Nuth dance club, Joatinga and Barra Shopping mall.

INT´L AIRPORT

BUS STATION

MARACANA

TIJUCA

SANTA TER

CORCOVADO
(CHRIST STATUE)

HUMAITA

GAVEA

LAGOA

LEBLON

IPANEMA

BARRA

SÃO CONRADO

Map not drawn to proportion

CITY OF RIO AT A GLANCE

REGIONAL AIRPORT

LAPA

GLORIA

FLAMENGO

BOTAFOGO

SUGAR LOAF AND URCA

LEME

COPACABANA

Downtown

From a tourist's point of view, the downtown area is a zone of interest due to its historic and cultural buildings (museums, churches, colonial architecture etc.) Although very active during the day, the downtown area (with the exception of Lapa and a few happy hours), is shady at night.

South Zone

The South Zone is the richer and prettier part of the city, with dozens of hills and mountains, the lagoon (Lagoa), and marvelous beaches. It is also safer than other areas, but care must be taken in the slums covering its hills. It is in the south zone where most of your day tours and nightlife will take place, so this is the area where we most recommend staying.

WHAT TO BRING

SUMMER CLOTHES

It is constantly hot and humid during and around the summer months, where you may not even want to wear a pair of pants, let alone a sweater at night. Ladies stick to flood pants, skirts, summer dresses and tank tops and T-shirts. Men stick to sandals, Bermuda shorts and T-shirts.

WINTER CLOTHES

Winter (June to August) in Rio feels like mid May in the northern part of the US and Europe or like beginning of April in the southern part of the US and Europe. Dress accordingly. During a cold night in mid winter, temperatures drop to 60F, 15C

EQUIPMENT

Sunglasses

Cheap watch

Digital camera (the smallest possible)

Disposable camera (for street events)

Anti-diarrhea medication

Sun-screen

Cap

GSM MOBILE PHONE

A GSM ready cellular phone will help you stay connected with the world by using the roaming service from Brazilian carriers. If your phone has a built-in camera, even better: take and send pictures and videos to make all your friends instantaneously jealous. (To learn how to activate your phone in Brazil, see page 32)

BUDGET AND MONEY

Cheap spending (eating at the hostel, few restaurants, no hard-core clubbing, basic tours): US$40 a day.

Average spending (restaurants and street food, hostel or cheap hotel, most of the tours): US$90 a day

All-out living (nice hotel, restaurants, all the tours, clubbing, shopping, massages etc): US$160 a day

You should bring half of your budget in cash and have the other half available on your credit card. Forget travellers checks as they are not readily accepted.

WHAT YOU DON'T NEED TO BRING

Towel or swimming gear

Snorkel or Hawaiian shirts

Winter jacket

Laptop

PETTY CASH

If you are in a group, instead of each person paying for their beer, for the taxi, their entrance and other small stuff, why not choose someone to carry the petty cash. Each morning, each member chips in R$50...

IDS AND CARDS

Passport

Student ID

Driver's License

Tourist Visa

2 Credit Cards (Visa & Mastercard) Call your card and let them know you'll be travelling to South America, as they sometimes freeze your card (on seeing irregular activity) till you call in to explain.

BEFORE FLYING TO BRAZIL

Call the closest Brazilian consulate and check with them on the required vaccines and visas. Also check the listing of consulates world-wide at:
www.brazil.org.uk

Joatinga Beach (pg. 36)

Rio For Partiers

10 RIO COMMANDMENTS

1 DO STAY IN ZONA SUL

Trust us on this: most of your day and night life will revolve around the Ipanema neighborhood. Try to stay as close to it as possible.

2 DON'T WALK AROUND WITH JEWELRY

Ladies and gentlemen! This is not your turf, so no matter how much clout you have at home, it is not worth shit here. Necklaces, rings, expensive watches, bracelets etc. are not to be worn except when you are off to a swanky event or club. Otherwise, keep it down low.

3 DON'T ARGUE WITH COPS

The cops here are instructed to take action as opposed to discussing who is right. It doesn't matter who is right, who stole what from whom, or if you didn't know she was under 18. If they want to arrest you for anything, let them, then call your consulate. If they want to fine you for something you did, usually for a driving offense, (another reason to not drive), then it is up to your slickness to implore them out of giving you a ticket.

4 GET CHANGE FOR A 50

The surest way to end up in hell is to walk around with a R$50 note thinking that the beer guy, the bus or taxi will have change. Whenever at a restaurant, shop or bar, pay with the R$50. Five R$10 bills can be worth more than a R$50.

5 DON'T TRY TO DO CULTURAL STUFF IN BARRA

Barra is a nice neighborhood in Rio. It is modeled on American suburbs, with wide avenues, malls and strip malls, yet with skyscraper residential buildings instead of houses. Most of the businesses have names in English. It is, in summary, a taste of American life. We do, however, recommend Pepe beach and Nuth dance club.

6 DON'T STAY FAR AWAY BECAUSE IT IS CHEAPER

Okay, you have a Brazilian connection you met back home or on the Internet. He is the one who begged you to come and you did. After arriving, you realize he lives in bumble fuck. What to do? Stay at his place and please him rather than enjoy the practicality of staying in Ipanema, as this Guide suggests? Or should you tell him that you want to explore Rio by yourself during the day (while he works or goes to school) and that you two can hook-up at night? Go for the second option. You will waste more time on cab traveling to and from his place.

7 DON'T TRY TO DRIVE

Don't rent a car and try to figure out Brazilian road signs. Ok, believe this: not even Cariocas (people from Rio) know how to get around this maze-like city. So unless you've got a very good excuse, don't try to drive around. One wrong turn and you can end up in the slums, being fined by the cops, or stuck in rush hour traffic. Even if your trip is all-expenses-paid, stick to taxis.

8 DON'T TRY THE PEPPERS

I beg you! Your stomach is not used to the chemistry in Brazilian peppers. Even if you can handle them, your intestines are bound to react in an explosive way for days, ruining your trip.

9 AVOID THE HILLS.

Most of Rio's slums are on the hills, so with the exception of Santa Teresa, Cosme Velho and Joatinga, hill sides and mountains should be avoided for your safety. Only go on trails with a tour guide.

10 DON'T ASSUME THE WEATHER WILL STAY NICE

The weather in Rio, as in most tropical cities, can change drastically within an hour. If it's sunny, don't waste your time doing indoor tours like museums or shopping.

WHERE TO STAY

If you are here more for the nightlife and beach, stay in Ipanema. If you are here for traditional daytime tourism, go with Copacabana, which is closer to most of the attractions and offers "Yes-now-I'm-on-vacation" ocean views. If you can't find anything affordable, opt for Botafogo, Flamengo or Gloria and Santa Teresa, which are all excellent options, despite being 20 minutes from Ipanema beach. If you can't find anywhere else, stay in a motel just off of Leblon. Just so you know, motels are not for truckers but for lovers, so the rooms are cheesy-swank, with jacuzzi, ceiling mirror, sauna and ocean views. And free condoms! For a list of motels, check page 120.

Ipanema

❶ Caesar Park (5★)
Av. Vieira Souto 460
reservas.cprj@caesarpark.com.br
www.caesar-park.com
2525-2525
rooms start at US$200 (low-season)

❸ Ipanema Inn (3★)
2523-6092 or 2511-5094
www.riodejaneiroguide.com/hotel/ip-anema_inn.htm
arpoador@unisys.com.br

❺ Sol Ipanema (4★)
Av. Vieira Souto, 320
2525-2020 or 22478484
www.solipanema.com.br/
reservas@solipanema.com.br

❷ Everest Rio (4★)
Rua Prudente de Moraes 1117
2525-2200 or 2521-3198
www.everest.com.br
reservas@everestrio.com.br

❹ Mar Ipanema (3★)
Rua Visconde de Pirajá 539
3875-9191
maripanema@maripanema.com
www.maripanema.com

❻ Arpoador Inn (3★)
Rua Francisco Otaviano 177
2523-6092 or 2511-5094
www.riodejaneiroguide.com/hotel/arpoa-dor_inn.htm
arpoador@unisys.com.br

Brazil country code = 55, Rio city code = 21

Stuff Near Ipanema

The commercial zone is along Visconde Street. The young beach spot is within a block's radius of the 9 lifeguard Post (Posto 9). Ipanema is extremely safe day and night.

Rio
Centro

South Zone

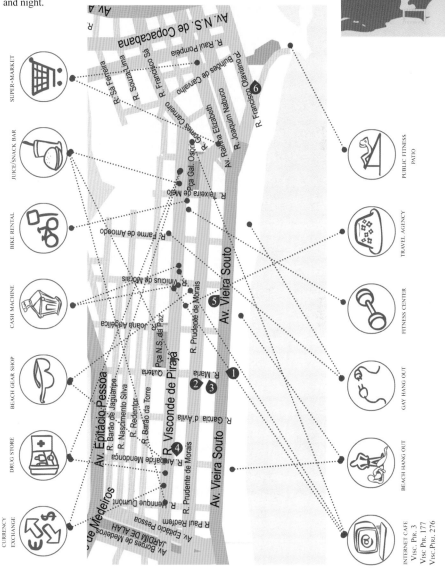

SUPER-MARKET

JUICE/SNACK BAR

BIKE RENTAL

CASH MACHINE

BEACH GEAR SHOP

DRUG STORE

CURRENCY EXCHANGE

PUBLIC FITNESS
PATIO

TRAVEL AGENCY

FITNESS CENTER

GAY HANG OUT

BEACH HANG OUT

INTERNET CAFE
VISC. PIR. 3
VISC. PIR. 177
VISC. PIR. 276

Av. N.S. de Copacabana
R. Raul Pompeia
R. Bulhões de Carvalho
R. Francisco Otaviano
R. Sá Ferreira
R. Souza Lima
R. Francisco Sá
R. Gomes Carneiro
Av. Rainha Elizabeth
Av. Joaquim Nabuco
R. Teixeira de Melo
Pça Gal. Osório
R. Farme de Amoedo
R. Vinícius de Morais
R. Prudente de Morais
Av. Vieira Souto
Joana Angélica
Pça N.S. da Paz
R. Maria Quitéria
R. Maria
R. Garcia d'Ávila
Av. Epitácio Pessoa
R. Barão de Jaguaripe
R. Nascimento Silva
R. Redentor
R. Barão da Torre
R. Aníbal de Mendonça
Av. Henrique Dumont
R. Prudente de Morais
R. Visconde de Piraja
Av. Vieira Souto
Av. Borges de Medeiros
JARDIM DE ALAH
Av. Epitácio Pessoa
R. Paul Redfern

Copacabana South

1 SOFITEL (5★)
Av. Atlântica 4240
2525-1206
www.sofitel.com.br
sofitelrio@accorhotels.com.br

3 Augusto's (4★)
Rua Bolivar 119
2547-1800
www.augustoshotel.com.br
reservas@augustoshotel.com.br

5 Portinari (4★)
Rua Francisco Sá 17
3222-8800
www.portinaridesignhotel.com.br/
reservas@hotelportinari.com.br

2 South American (4★)
Rua Francisco Sá 90
reservas@southamericanhotel.com.br
www.southamericanhotel.com.br
2227-9161

4 Miramar Palace (4★)
Av. Atlantica 3668
reservas.miramar@windsorhoteis.com.br
www.windsorhoteis.com
2195-6200 or 0800 232-211

6 Martinique (3★)
Av. Sá Ferreira 30
reservas.martinique@windsorhoteis.com.br
www.windsorhoteis.com
2195-5200

Stuff Near Copa South

This side of Copacabana is privileged by being close to Ipanema. It has two busy streets, N.S. Copacabana and Barata Ribeiro, where most shops can be found. The beach is the third best in Zona Sul, after Ipanema and Leblon, packed with gringos, beach vendors and a few obvious hookers.

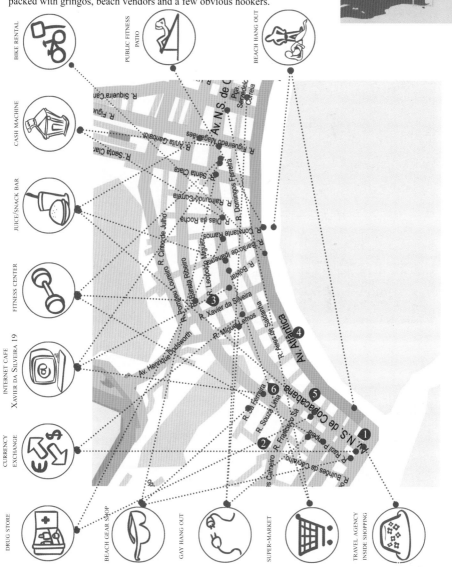

Copacabana North

❶ JW Marriott Hotel (5★)
Av. Atlântica 2600
2545 6500 or toll free 0800 703 1512
www.marriott.com/riomc
reservas.brasil@marriott.com

❸ Grandarrell Ouro Verde (4★)
Av. Atlântica 1.456
2543-4123
www.dayrell.com.br
ouroverde@dayrell.com.br

❺ Plaza Copacabana (4★)
Av. Princesa Isabel 263
2195-5500 or 2543-8071
www.windsorhoteis.com.br
reservas.plaza@windsorhoteis.com.br

❷ Oceano Copacabana (4★)
Rua Hilário de Gouveia 17
2548-4260
www.oceanohotel.com.br
oceanocophotel@oceanohotel.com

❹ Excelsior Copacabana (4★)
Av. Atlantica 1800
2195-5800 or 0800-704287
reservas.excelsior@windsorhoteis.com.br
www.windsorhoteis.com

❻ Ibiza Copacabana (3★)
Rua Belfort Roxo 250
2295-7887
www.ibizacopacabanahotel.com.br/
ibiza.copacabana@uol.com.br

Stuff Near Copa North

Copacabana North is a good option if you want to stay close to downtown and the main tourist attractions. It is just as busy during the day, but quieter than the south part of Copa at night. It is also a little more dangerous at night, so cab back and forth for any distance longer than a few blocks.

Rio Centro

South Zone

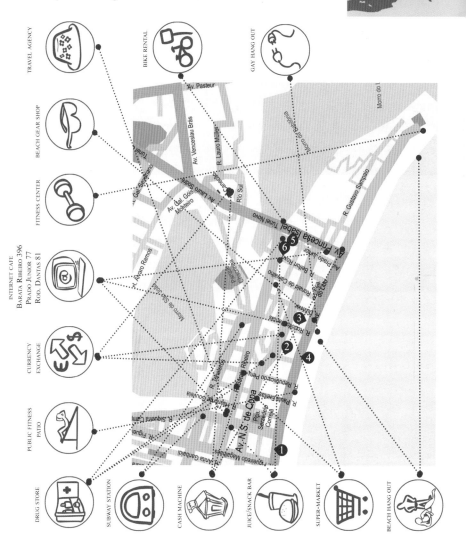

TRAVEL AGENCY

BIKE RENTAL

GAY HANG OUT

BEACH GEAR SHOP

FITNESS CENTER

INTERNET CAFE
BARATA RIBEIRO 396
PRADO JUNIOR 77
ROD. DANTAS 81

CURRENCY EXCHANGE

PUBLIC FITNESS PATIO

DRUG STORE

SUBWAY STATION

CASH MACHINE

JUICE/SNACK BAR

SUPER-MARKET

BEACH HANG OUT

Around Rio

ER

LEBLON

Marina Palace (5★)
Av. Delfim Moreira, 630
reservas@hotelmarina.com.br
www.hotelmarina.com.br
2172-1000

BARRA

Windsor Barra (4★)
Av. Sernambetiba, 2630
reservas.windsorbarra@windsorhoteis.com.br
www.windsorhoteis.com.br
2195-5000

SÃO CONRADO

Intercontinental (5★)
Av. Prefeito Mendes de Morais, 222
reservas@inter-rio.com.br
www.intercontinental.com
3323-2200

LEBLON

Sheraton (5★)
Av. Niemayer 121
reservas.rio@sheraton.com
www.sheraton-rio.com
2529-1122

BARRA

Sheraton Barra (5★)
Av. Lúcio Costa 3150
reservas.barra@sheraton.com
www.sheraton-barra.com.br
3139-8000

SANTA DE TERESA

Solar do Santa Guesthouse
Ladeira do Meirelles, 32
reservas@solardesanta.com
www.solardesanta.com
2221-2117

Brazil country code = 55, Rio city code = 21

Hotel Alternatives

GETTING THE BEST DEALS

Whatever you do, don't show up in Rio and expect the reception to give a huge discount just because it's low season. They won't. They can't as it is part of their pricing strategy. To get the best deals, contact either the hotel or a travel agency in advance asking them where they would stay for the budget you have. They won't try to dump a bad deal on you because they know you have probably sent a few emails around with the same request. Most will try to get you the best deal they can find from a hotel they have inspected to also conquer you as their customer for other services or packages.

You can also use our quote request tool, that sends your request to a few hotel booking agencies from one form:
www.rioforpartiers.com/planning.html

WHY RENT AN APARTMENT?

The best option if you are coming with a group is to rent an apartment, since most apartments for rent are 3 bedroom, fitting everyone comfortably. Most have doormen, maid service (US$20 for day's cleaning and laundry), TV, DVD etc. Some may even have beach gear, like bodyboards, surfboards or bikes. Prices vary according to the usual apt factors, so the range is from US$50 for a one-bedroom to US$500 for a beach view 4 bedroom penthouse.

APARTMENT RENTAL
LUXURY

Rent in Rio
56 Apartments spread all over Ipanema and Copacabana allow you to pick the right sized apt in the right location at the right price. Many penthouses.
Dan Babush
dbreport@aol.com
www.rentinrio.com
US 1-877-289-7543 or Rio 3523-0313
Inquire for discounts to RFP readers

BUDGET

Rio Charm
Dozens of apartments around Ipanema and Copacabana, all very affordable.
info@riocharm.com
8606-7497
US 305 767-4525
www.riocharm.com
Inquire about discounts to RFP readers

WHY STAY IN A HOSTEL?

The best solution for those willing to part with comfort in exchange for savings. Hostels tend to be 4 to 8 guests bunked up per room, which leads to lots of sociability while detracting your privacy. If you are travelling alone, you'll group up within minutes of your check-in and start making travel and drinking buddies. Some older travellers like the sociability so much they sleep in hotels but get a room in a hostel to participate in the various group tours and parties.

HOSTEL

Che Lagarto Ipanema
If you want to hang with the party people, this is it: a brand new well located hostel with the feel of a hotel, close to lots of bars and restaurants, lots of great services, internet cafe and bar inside.
Rua Paul Redfern 48
www.chelagarto.com

GENERAL

5 Concierge Tips to Fun in Rio

By Roberta Bezerra*

1 - Sunsets... If you are in Ipanema around sunset time, just run to the beach, it's amazing to watch the sunset from the beach and when it's done everyone applauds it, so join in.

2 - Eat... Rio caters all different foods and tastes, so it's the perfect place to take a few pounds back home, eat a lot of all our different food, drink caipirinhas and never miss the desserts.

3 - Shop... shoes, clothes, jewelry... Our shopping malls are wonderful, while shopping stop for a moment and ask for a *cafezinho* e *pão de queijo* (coffee and cheese bread) I bet you won't regret it.

4 - Dance... Rio has all Brazilian rhythms, you can dance Samba, Forró and so much more, ask the Concierge where you can go learn to dance, so when you are back home you can show some moves to your friends.

5 - Always ask the Concierge.... If you are lost, or almost lost, if you want to know where to buy, where to eat, where to have fun, the concierges from any hotel will always be at your disposal to show you the best of Rio !

*Roberta Bezerra is the proud President of Les Clefs d'Or Brésil. The Les Clefs d'Or concierges are trained to guide, inform, and advise visitors throughout their hotel stays. Les Clefs d'Or concierges pride themselves in learning about their cities and environs, restaurants, theatre engagements, events, and sightseeing destinations in order to help guests get the most out of their visits.

Tours

3 THINGS TO ASK BEFORE BOOKING A TOUR

1: What happens in case of rain? Postponed or carried out anyway?

2: How long does it take to pick up others in the tour?

3: Is it possible to find transportation back if I break away from the group?

4: Will there be food vendors and restaurants involved or should I pack some snacks?

Don`ts

Don`t get irate with Brazilians who show up half an hour late... that`s within reason in Rio. Its called Brazilian time. Salvador time is even worse!

Don`t ride in the front seats of buses or vans... they drive too fast.

Don`t forget to double check any info you get on the street: Brazilians are always glad to help, even with wrong info.

TIPS

Rio By Yourself

Want to meet others to make the most of your visit? Use these tricks and team up.

1) JOIN A GROUP TOUR:

- Soccer game
- Schooner tour
- Favela tour
- Hiking

2) ASK A TRAVEL AGENT:

Whoever booked your hotel, apt or flight can introduce you to others who are in Rio by themselves, so you can make some vacation buddies.

3) HIT THE HAPPY HOURS EARLY.

Why not, right? Should make you more extroverted by the time people arrive.

4) ASK YOUR CONCIERGE.

They should know who else is staying at your hotel that shares common interests or wants to split a tour, like renting a speed boat, private city tour etc.

5) JOIN A SMALL NIGHTLIFE TOUR

Ask before about the group dynamics.

How to cure a hangover

A nasty hangover can ruin your next day. Follow these and you`ll be back at the bar by 2pm.

1) Before going to bed drunk, drink as much water as possible.

2) Aleve, Tylenol or any powerful aspirin in the morning.

3) Drink some coconut water the next morning. 2 coconuts if you are normal sized, 1 if you are short, 3 if your nick name is Shrek.

4) A beef pastel (turn-over) or a picanha burger with fries are just what the doctor ordered.

5) Jog and sweat it away. What better place to do it other than the beach bike path (for joggers too).

To avoid hangovers

1) Don`t drink caipirinhas made on the street... they tend to use unfiltered ice.

2) Pace your drinking with a glass of water every so often. (I`ve never been able to remember to do this, but hypothetically it makes sense.)

3) Before going back to the hotel, throw down a steak sandwich from Lammas or Cervantes (check page 120). I have no idea if this works, but it sure tastes good.

4) Ask for premium *cachaça* or vodka when ordering your *caipirinha*. The cheap brands are not as filtered or selectively distilled.

5) A shot of olive oil before drinking will help you win any binging competition...really!

6) Cut yourself off after 17 caipirinhas... I mean, you gotta have limits, man!

GETTING

Getting around in Rio is easy: just get in a cab! 1 out of every 3 cars is a taxi (or so it seems). What's more: it's cheap. You can go from downtown to Ipanema for about R$20 (US$10). From Ipanema to Barra for about the same. Just remember to ask the taxi driver if he knows how to get to where you want to go before you step in "voce sabe chegar no …. " pronounced "vo-say sa-bee shay-gar no [insert place here]…". If he doesn't know, take the next cab.

FRESCAO

A safe and comfortable option if you are going to or from the downtown area is to take the "Frescao", an air conditioned passenger bus that serves the business commuters.

They go for R$5 and run more frequently during rush hours.

CAR RENTALS

Renting a car is not a good option unless you have a Brazilian escort who will be driving you around. It does become helpful if you are planning on visiting Buzios, Petropolis and Paraty (cars are not allowed in Ilha Grande).

CHAUFFEUR SERVICE

The classy option is always chauffeur service, available outside 5 star hotels. Although their rates start at R$70 an hour, some chauffeur services are also accredited tour guides, making them an excellent alternative to guided tours.
Marcelo Esteves (UK,ES)
9984-7654 or marafes@terra.com.br

VANS

Another option, if you master a little Portuguese or some Spanish, is to ride the vans on the beach routes. For R$4, you can go from Ipanema to Barra. Of course, if you are in a group of 4, you are better off taking a cab.

Just signal a van that has the name of the neighborhood you

are heading to, shuffle your way in and tell the driver when he should let you out.

SUBWAY

Of course, there is also the subway, which is very fast and convenient for those traveling between downtown and Copacabana.

BUSES

The other less recommended transportation method is the public buses. Although a lot cheaper, these take longer (up to 55 minutes from downtown to Ipanema, where a cab would take 20 minutes) and are riskier, as crooks have been robbing buses, and the mob sets one or two on fire when angry at the government.

AROUND

BUS AND SUBWAY MAP

Between Downtown and
Copacabana, Ipanema and Leblon

▬▬ ▬▬ 474

Between Downtown and Gloria,
Catete, Flamengo, Botafogo,
Humaita, Jd. Botânico and Gavea

▬▬ ▬▬ 438

Between Tijuca, Maracana,
Downtown and Copacabana
▬ ▬ ▬ SUBWAY

THINGS YOU'LL

How to Stay in Touch with Home

Your GSM mobile works in Brazil. It roams calls using local carriers, so you can send text messages, pictures, videos, access the internet, and, of course, make and receive calls. We recommend using TIM's service since they have the largest GSM coverage in Brazil. To activate TIM's roaming service on your phone, simply go to:
Phone settings >> Manual network selection >> TIM BRASIL or 72402 or BRARN or BRA02

To make calls in Rio, use the following dialing process:
• **Making local calls: simply dial the number**

• **Calls within Brazil: 0 + long distance carrier code (TIM's is 41) + city code + phone number**

• **Calls outside Brazil: 00 + international long distance carrier code (TIM's is 41) + country code + phone number**

Your contacts back home can reach you simply by dialing your regular number, with no prefixes.

To contact TIM's multi-lingual customer care, dial: *144 from your phone or 0800 741 4141 from any phone in Brazil.

Brazilian money:

At the airport, be sure to change US$50, enough to pay for the cab to your hotel, where you'll be able to exchange at fairer rates.

At the Beach Gear Shop

Flip Flops

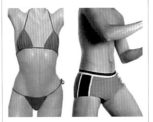

Brazilian fashion beach wear

After-sun lotion (Aloe Vera)

Frescobol paddles (optional)

At the pharmacy

Sun-screen

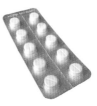

Antidiarrheal medicine
"remedio para desarranjo"

Disposable camera

NEED TO GET

Hangover medicine
"remedio para ressaca"

AT THE SUPER-MARKET

Toilet paper

Bottled water

Snacks

WITH THE STREET VENDORS

Cheap watch

Calling card (found at the news-stands, roughly R$5)

Cheap Sunglasses

CARRY AT ALL TIMES

Reals (Pronounced "Hey-ice") in small bills

Photo ID (or a xerox of your passport)

1 VISA credit card

WHAT TO DO

READ THIS BOOK

During your first day at the beach, while you wait for a butt to pass by, read this book! It will guarantee you a great time, and lots of savings.

FRESCOBOL

The paddle ball game the Cariocas play is one of the few non-competitive sports in the world. Stand 15ft (5m.) apart, close to the water, and paddle away.

BODY SURF

Body surfing is probably the purest water sport in the world. That means you can have fun with nature without any equipment, even swimming trunks. As a wave is passing you by, jump with it, do two strokes so your body catches up to the speed of the wave, and ride the wake.

BEER

Hey! Now we're talking! Beer drinking at the beach is everybody's favorite sport. But do drink some water every now and then, as you are probably dehydrating faster than you think, which will make you sleepy by dusk.

JOG

Feel like exercising or sweating off yesterday's hangover? Jog along the beach. No further explaining needed…

BODY-WATCH

Inevitable.

WALK

Duh…

VOLLEYBALL

Yes, you want to play volleyball. But the Cariocas playing it won't even recognize the fact that you are waiting to be asked in. You can either be persistent and ask someone in-between games, or you can rent or borrow a ball from someone and play on an empty court (unlikely to happen on weekends). If you can hang with the best or if you are tall, they may let you in. If you suck, practice elsewhere.

AT THE BEACH

SOCCER – FOOTBALL

In most cases, since the teams run from 4 to as many as 16 players on each side, you can just ask anyone of the team players if you can join their game. This is if you can hang. If you can't, go back to paddle ball.

MASSAGE

You can get a beach massage with any of the masseurs posted every 6 blocks close to the sidewalk. Their prices range from R$50 to R$80 an hour.

What not to do

DON'T TRY THE BEACH SHRIMP

Or any beach seafood. Certain death.

DON'T MAKE EYE CONTACT WITH THE VENDORS

If you do, they will come and pester you for several minutes. When they catch your attention, quickly give them the no sign by shaking you index finger just twice.

GUYS: DON'T LIE DOWN ON THE SAND

That's for women or guys accompanied by their girlfriends.

DON'T FORGET TO TAKE OFF YOUR SUNGLASSES

Raccoon eyes are not cool in Rio.

DON'T LEAVE YOUR STUFF UNGUARDED

When going into the water, simply ask your beach neighbor to watch your stuff for you. If you brought a digital camera or any amount of money, one of your group should stay behind.

Water safety tips

Whenever a fierce wave is coming your way, you should swim towards it so you can jump through it before it breaks on you.

If it does break in front of you, drop to the bottom, stay as close to the sand as possible and wait for it to pass over you.

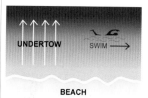

BEACH

If you get caught in the undertow (or any water current pulling you out to sea), two simple rules: 1) don't struggle against it. 2) swim parallel to the beach till you are out of the current.

If there are more than a few surfers in the ocean, try to stay as far from them as possible. One slip and their board cracks your head open (sorry about the drama).

If you can't swim you should stay close to the life guard posts; in case you get pulled out.

DAY TOURS

Here is the digested version:

If you want to try a little of everything, this is what we recommend:

Day 1: Sit on Ipanema beach all day and unwind.

Day 2: Do a bike tour from Copacabana to Glória, stopping to go up Sugar Loaf.

Day 3: Santa Teresa and Corcovado.

Day 4: Hang-glide or paraglide, followed by a tour in a favelas.

Day 5: A cultural tour of downtown, Christ statue at sunset.

Day 6: Eco-tourism hiking tour.

Day 7: Diving in the Cagarras Islands.

Day 8: (or Saturday): Joatinga beach, followed by body boarding lessons at Pepe beach in Barra.

Day 9: (or Sunday): Ipanema beach. Maracanã at 5pm.

Relax: Ipanema

The first thing anyone arriving in Rio should do is sit on Ipanema beach for at least a few hours. But of course, you can't just go to the beach - there is a little ritual to follow. Estimate Total Time (T): 8h Estimated Total Cost (C): R$ 130   Best on: Sunny Weekday

❶ BEACH GEAR

First, buy yourself some fashion conscious swimming gear as Brazilian beach fashion is different from other countries': swimming trunks are wide on the side, and bikinis are medium-small triangles with a horizontal straps.
Garota de Ipanema
Rua Vinicius de Moraes 53

❷ BREAKFAST

Then go for a juice and "pastel" (see page 144) at any of the juice bars on Visconde de Pirajá street.

❸ IPANEMA BEACH

You can now finally go to the beach. A beach tent vendor will find a chair for you upon request (R$2 to R$3). Plunk down and let the view sink in. Don't order a beer just yet. Butt-watch instead.

You are in one of the world's most gifted cities, and you are on vacation. Now you can order a beer. Ask for a beer holder ("isopor") as the heat can warm up your beer before you get half way through it.

You can try most of the

Drink Mate w/ lemonade: A must

Rio For Partiers

Ipanema girls

stuff the beach vendors have to offer, with the exception of the shrimp, which tends to go bad under the sun.

If you want to try something different, look for "Uruguai's" beach tent. He makes probably the best chicken sandwiches in Rio, using his own "chimichuri" sauce. Don't add the peppers though.

Another good option is the

hotdog from any of the two vendors.

After the beach, wash off the sand at the lifeguard post and head over to Benkei (sushi) (A), Garota de Ipanema (steak and fries) (B), Delírio Tropical (salads) (C), Big Nectar (sandwiches) (D) for a late lunch.

4 EMAIL

Walk across to Visconde and check your email at the closest internet cafe. Be sure to visit the

updates section of our site:
www.rioforpartiers.com/updates.html

WINDOW BROWSE VISCONDE

Check out the shops along Visconde de Piraja, walking counter traffic till sundown. Cut across to the beach to hopefully catch the sunset in Ipanema, drink in hand. Head back to the hotel for a siesta.

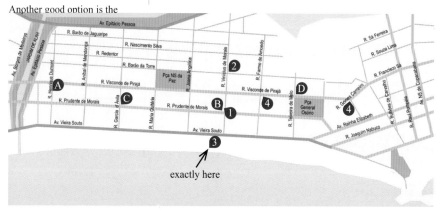

exactly here

Relax: Pão de Açúcar & Schooner

Although these neighborhoods don't offer much to do, they offer a lot to see: Flamengo, Botafogo bay and Urca with Sugar Loaf. Visit Sugar Loaf, followed by a schooner boat tour. Est.Total Time (T): 8h Est. Total Cost (C): R$100   Best on: Sunny Weekday

1 BREAKFAST

Start off with an açaí and pastel at any juice bar close to where you are staying.

2 SUGAR LOAF

Cab to Urca by 11am. Catch a cable car to the two peaks. Take your time, but around noon you should start heading down for lunch.

3 LUNCH AT PORCÃO

Cab towards "Porção Rios" our favorite churrascaria, situated in Flamengo park, overlooking the bay, Niteroi and Sugar Loaf. At 2:20pm you should be on a cab to the Marina da Gloria.

4 SUNSET SCHOONER BOAT TRIP

SPECIAL DEAL FOR OUR READERS CHECK BACK FLAP

Once you get to the Gloria Marina, look for the Marlin Yacht Shop, which offers the 2 hour schooner tour which leaves at 3pm. For R$50 Marlin Yacht (page 48) will take you on a traditional Brazilian sail boat around the Guanabara Bay, hopefully catching the sunset.

Marlin Yacht Boat Rental
Contact: Roberto tel: 9986-9678
marlin@marlinyacht.com.br
www.marlinyacht.com.br

View of Pão de Açucar (Sugar Loaf Mountain and
Botafogo bay from Corcovado (Christ Statue)

Relax: Joatinga & Barra Beaches

Joatinga is one of Rio's cutest, yet most hidden, beaches. It is only visited by locals during weekends or during weekdays in January, when surfers are on school vacation.

Est. Total Time (T): 7h   Est. Total Cost (C): R$ 80   Best on: Sunny Weekend

1 BREAKFAST

A *suco de mamão* with a *kibe* or *misto quente* at your closest juice bar.

2 JOATINGA

After breakfast at your favorite juice bar, hop into a Cab and ask for Joatinga. Although the cab fare may be expensive (Ipanema to Joatinga=R$16), it will make sense once you check out the view from up above.

Walk down the precarious path to the beach. There are one or two beach tents to offer you chairs and drinks. They charge more than others because of the remote location. Shadows are cast early, due to the stone walls around Joatinga, so once that happens (usually around 3:30),

get back up and call a taxi from the nearest phone booth, or ask a Brazilian with cellular to dial 2434-0553 and call a cab for you.

3 PEPE BEACH

Take it to Praia do Pepe in Barra. Once there just sit on the sand and for the next few hours checking out the hard-bodied people around you.

At sundown, head two blocks west towards the Republica

Gourmet restaurant for a late lunch. Get a cab and head back home.

If you also want to visit other famous distant beaches, like Grumari, Prainha or Itacoatiara, we suggest you get a guided tour and save money on taxi.

Rio Charm Tours
Contact: Bryan
8606-7497 or info@riocharm.com
www.riocharm.com
Prices for guided car tours roughly R$70 per hour

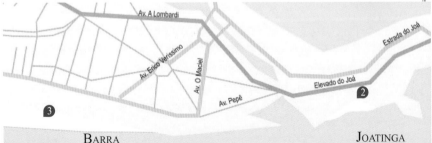

BARRA   JOATINGA

Relax: Copacabana

Copacabana still remains a place of Brazilian ethnic, cultural and social diversity. This alone makes it all interesting. Est.Total Time (T): 8h Est. Total Cost (C): R$ 130   Best on: Sunny Weekday

❶ BREAKFAST

Start off with a hearty breakfast (in case you missed yours at your hotel) at Colombo, in the Copacabana Fort, on the extreme right of the beach, where you can absorb the view. R$2 to enter to the fort.

❷ POSTO 6

Walk to the beach an get a chair and bask in the sun for a few.

❸ WALK AND WATCH

After this, you can walk up and down Copacabana's sidewalks.

❹ LATE LUNCH

Once you get to IberoStar Hotel, head in three blocks and ask for Cervantes. Sit down at "Galeto Sats" (the grungy restaurant next to Cervantes) and there you will enjoy another Brazilian meal: game hen in lemon sauce. Ask for "*batata portuguesa*" as a side dish, *farofa*, *pao de alho* and "vinaigrette".

❺ MASSAGE

After your lunch, walk along Copacabana beach looking for a shiatsu massage specialist. They do a great job at a cheap rate (roughly $60 an hour).

❻ LOUNGE

Then head over to Modern Sound, one of Rio's largest and most complete record stores. They have a good happy hour there every day, although it can sometimes be packed with older people. Since it's free, it is worth checking out.

EMAIL

Check you email next door and head back to your hotel.

Relax: Soccer Game at Maracanã

Wimbledon to tennis, Madison Square Garden to basketball, Maracanã to soccer. An extremely exciting experience. Est. Total Time (T): 4h Est. Total Cost (C): R$ 60   Best on: Sundays

MARACANÃ

Once inside, you'll experience Rio at its most religious: 100K+ people individually stopping to whole-heartedly pray for their teams. Moments after "Amen", you'll be playing "simon says" for the next two hours: a little guy acting like a maestro sitting all the way down there will be showing 10,000 fans what to do, sing and shout. This is called an "organized fanhood" since that faction of fans all have their chants, stadium sized flags and sneaked-in fireworks. The most common chants involve the judge's ass or mother. Once a goal is scored everyone gets an orgasm and the chants get re-energized. If you see the beer vendor, get 2 as they are scarce. After the game, stick together to go home.

To go with safe guides and a large group of young travellers (great mingling), call these guys.
Brazil Expedition
Contact: Eduardo
tel: 9998-2907
www.brazilexpedition.com
tours@brazilexpedition.com

Price: R$70 = Soccer game at Maracanã with tickets & transfer. Every Sunday, occasionally on Wednesdays.

Maracanã, still the world's largest stadium, officially capable of holding 120,000 people, yet it has seen over 180,000 at some popular soccer finals.

SOCCER GAME

As soon as you get to Rio, ask around to see if there is a game going on and if it will be good: meaning big teams or championship finals. This will be an experience like you never had. Needless to say, the average IQ at any moment is below 60 (group average or cumulative), so don't look forward to a "good-ol British soccer riot".

BREAKFAST

First you will need a strong breakfast. It may include beer, since you will be pounding them in the next 30 minutes.

TAILGATING

After the good boys from Brazil Expedition pick you up from your hotel, you'll be taken to outside the stadium where you should get yourself a T-shirt of the team you will be rooting for (Flamengo, Botafogo, Fluminense and Vasco are the better two from Rio). Try the food vendors, even the fillet-meow, possibly made from street cats. The air is charged, as enthusiasm and hope are conjured on both sides.

RZ

Relax: Christ Statue & Santa Teresa

This is one of those days when you wake up on top of the world: First stop, Corcovado (Christ statue).

Est.Total Time (T): 6h Est. Total Cost (C): R$ 90 Best on: Visible Weekday

1 BREAKFAST

After breakfast get to your local fruit stand/ grocery store and buy one mango, one *caju* fruit and one *fruta do conde*, (we'll explain).

2 TREM DO CORCOVADO

Get a cab to the Trem do Corcovado, so you can take the train along a eye-opening track up to the statue. Rua do Cosme Velho 513, 8:30am to 18:30pm).

The taxi driver will try to tell you he can drive you up to the statue for X reais, but it is not the same as the train experience.

Once at the base of the Corcovado train, be sure to check out Zerrener's (our contributing photographer) photo store while waiting for the next departure.

3 CHRIST STATUE

Once up there check out the view, shoot photos, have a morning beer, hang out for an hour, then head back down.

4 SANTA TERESA

Cab to "Largo do Guimarães" in Santa Teresa. There you can catch a trolley heading towards Lapa. This tram runs through St. Teresa, a turn-of-the-century neighborhood filled with cute little houses in the traditional Portuguese post-colonial style.

5 LUNCH

Get off the tram at Largo do Guimarães (ask somebody) and sit for lunch at any of these places, whichever may be open: Sobrenatural, Bar do Mineiro, Simplesmente, Bar do Arnaudo. They all carry typical Brazilian dishes at fair prices.

6 LARGO DA CARIOCA

Hop back on the tram and get off at the last stop. Ask around for Largo da Carioca.

There you will find a nice bouquet of Brazilian wildlife: kiosks selling everything infringing on copyrights, fire-eaters, and circus freaks, etc. After checking the human zoo, head over to the Church Sao Francisco da Penitencia, one of Brazil's most beautiful Baroque churches.

7 HAPPY HOUR

You can then, as a reward, head over to Lapa and sit down at Beco do Rato for a dozen cold ones.

Corcovado Train climbing up to Christ statue

Rio For Partiers

Relax: Party Boat along the coast

Rio's coast includes several islands, beaches, bays, peninsulas etc, making you wish you could remember your geography lessons. A boat tour will see it all. Best on: Sunny Day

Another great idea, which isn't too expensive when compared to international prices, is to take an exclusive boat tour for you and your friends.

There are dozens of islands around Rio. A schooner boat is larger and more comfortable than speed boats. It can take you to different islands for snorkeling (like those in front of Ipanema, Cagarras islands), or across the bay to Niteroi's Itaipú beach, checking out forts along the way. You can anchor up and enjoy fried shrimp at the beach kiosks.

Boat rental services will include a licensed sailor, sea insurance, snorkels and a fridge full of ice for your beer. You should pass by the supermarket and get what you need. Do call upon arriving in Rio to be on stand-by as most boats get rented on weekends, as they need a few hours to get the boat ready and to check sea and weather conditions.

Marlin Yacht Boat Rental

Contact: Roberto tel: 9986-9678
marlin@marlinyacht.com.br
www.marlinyacht.com.br

SPECIAL DEAL
FOR OUR READERS
CHECK BACK FLAP

Party Boat Prices:4-6 hour private boat rental = starting from R$750. Includes 6 persons. For each additional add R$30.

Speed and sail boats also available.

Relax: Beach & Dunes Expedition

Ever wanted to go on the Paris-Dakar endurance race? Or to put your SUV under extreme conditions? With this tour, you can do so while abusing someone else's car.

You'll rough it taking dirt trails, crossing rivers, stopping at crystal water beaches for a splash, shooting photos from cliffs and living out Jeep commercials, in a Landrover.

SUN COAST HALF DAY

The driver, Horacio, will take three different off-road trails. The first one is a deeply rutted trail that leads to a waterfall in Sampaio Correia, where you'll trek a little. Then you'll go over dunes for some 4X4 fun. At the beaches you'll stop for a splash. Afterwards you'll have lunch at "Mineira", a flavourful country style restaurant. Before heading home, you'll pass by the Museum of Contemporary Art in Niteroi, shaped like a "flying saucer". Length: 7 hours.

SUN COAST FULL DAY

A full day version of the above tour, except that after the dunes you'll speed over several flat beaches on the way to Arraial do Cabo. There you'll have fresh seafood. Afterwards splashing at the crystal clear waters of Arraial, you'll go over some dunes to Itaipuacu. Afterwards, you'll take the road home. Length: 10 hours.

Hoca Tour
Contact: Horacio
9322-0870 or 3472-7576
www.hocatour.com.br
contato@hocatour.com.br
**Half-day trip: From R$200pp, call to reserve seat.
Full Day: From R$300pp.**

Relax: Helicopter tour of Rio

Rio is a memory-avalanche of all the geography lessons you were forced to sit through (without, of course, avalanches and glaciers).. Est.Total Time: 7min to 1h :: Est. Total Cost: R$ 150 to R$875pp Best on: Clear Day

Rio has ice-age-rounded mountains (yep, that's what made them smooth), peninsulas, bars, bays, rivers, lakes, islands, reefs, forests, shanty towns, grid and non-grid neighborhoods, forts, airports, ship yards, industrial districts, cumulous clouds stuck at a mountain and a giant Christ making sure everyone one is well-behaved.

There are several interesting tours that go over the main attractions, such as Sugar Loaf, Christ statue, Maracana, Lagoa, Tijuca forest, Copa & Ipanema.
Helisight
Sales: 2511-2141 or Lagoon: 2259-6995
or Sugar Loaf: 2542-7895
helisight@helisight.com.br
www.helisight.com.br

Price: **Route 1 (pink route) and 2 (blue)** = R$150 per person (6-7 mins)

Route 3 (yellow)= R$230 (8-9mins)
Other routes available

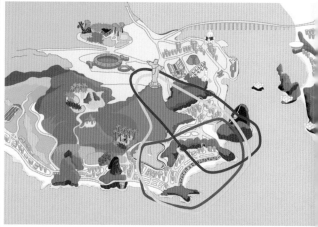

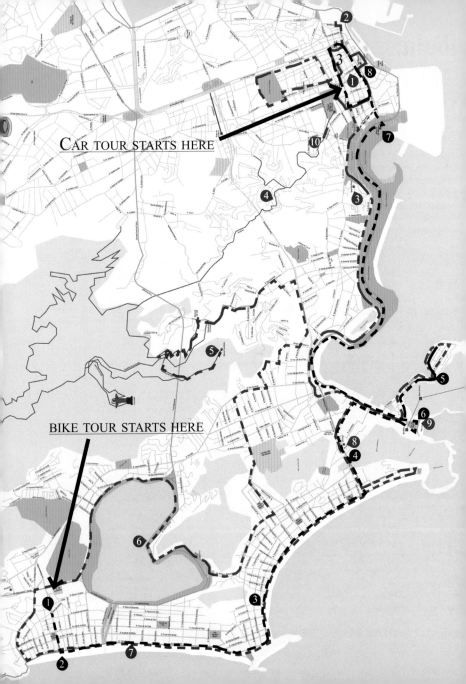

CAR TOUR STARTS HERE

BIKE TOUR STARTS HERE

Relax: "Do-It-All" 1 Day Tour

Bike Tour

You got one day and you want to see it all in a fun way: Rent a bike in Leblon

① BikeTech
Av. Bartolomeu Mitre 455, Leblon
2239-3600 or 2158-3340

and travel through the touristy spots of the city, that line the water front (with the exception of Christ statue), always heading for downtown.

Ride it to ② Leblon beach and along to Ipanema beach. Cut across to Copacabana ③, head towards Leme, then take the tunnel towards Botafogo ④ and head for Urca.

For lunch, have a "*Picanha Brasileira*" (sirloin on a skillet - eats 3 to 4) at Garota da Urca ⑤. Then take the cable cars up to Sugar Loaf ⑥, hang out for an hour. Continue your ride along Botafogo, Flamengo and Gloria beach.

Stop at the Modern Art Museum ⑦, lock up your bike and run around in the museum for 40 minutes. Hop back on, head downtown, quickly check out the Paço Imperial ⑧, then lock up the bikes and kick start the happy hour in Arco do Teles, right after the Paco Imperial.

Have a beer at any of the bars.

At 6 pm put your bike into the back of a station wagon taxi and return it before the rent-a-bike closes (8 pm).

Car Tour

Conversely, you can hire a taxi (you will need a Brazilian to bargain this part for you) for R$200 or a tour guide so they can take you to all the touristy spots, where you can step out, look around for 15 minutes, then proceed to the next.

Given that traffic will slow you down during rush hours, this is where we recommend you ask him to take you: Zig-zag all of down-town ①, Mosteiro de

São Bento ② (stop and visit for 15 minutes), Gloria Church ③ (stop and visit for 15 minutes), Santa Teresa ④ (ride along main street) and stop for lunch at Bar do Mineiro (Largo do Guimaraes).

Then continue to Dona Marta ⑤ (stop and appreciate the view for 30 minutes) , Lagoa ⑥ (drive around it) Ipanema ⑦ (sit at beach for an hour), Copacabana (walk along beach), Botafogo ⑧ (shop at Rio Sul till almost sundown), Pão de Açúcar ⑨ (go up during sundown), then head over to Lapa ⑩ for a *caipirinha* or two at any of the happy hours, then back to hotel or airport.

For private tour guides, call
Rio Charm Tours
8606-7497 or info@riocharm.com
www.riocharm.com

View of Sugar Loaf from National Airport.

Relax: Lagoa & Botanical Gardens

Cycling around Lagoa is a great option when the weather or your head is cloudy. Est. Total Time (T): 5h Est. Total Cost (C): R$ 60   Best on: Cloudy Weekday

❺ Parque Lage

Then bike over to Parque Lage, right next door. Nice. Snoop`s "Beautiful" video was taped there.

❶ Breakfast

Get breakfast at a juice bar: *Acai* with a ham&cheese sandwich (*misto*).

❷ Rent bike

Rent a bike for the whole day (R$35) at
BikeTech
Av. Bartolomeu Mitre, 455
2239-3600 or 2158-3340

Make sure you rent the lock too, as you will be leaving them locked here and there.

❸ Cycle around Lagoa

Head over to Lagoa and cycle around it anti-clockwise, stopping at any of the coconut stands for some coconut water.

❹ Jardim Botânico

Once three quarters of the way around it, you should look for signs of the Jardim Botanico. Get over there, lock the bikes and walk around for half an hour.

❻ Lunch

Then get back out and go for lunch at the Gavea mall`s food court. After lunch, check out the rest of Gavea Mall.

ADVENTURE SPORTS

With the exception of winter sports, you can find every mode of sport in Rio, from golfing to hang-gliding, from kite-surfing to cart racing.

Given that the price of playing these sports are about 1/3 of what you would pay in the 1st World, we highly recommend indulging in them during your stay.

All the guides and instructors listed here were chosen for their ability to serve tourists and to speak English and other languages. They all offer competitive rates and are certified by the state and/or their sports association.

We have not listed any traditional, indoor or Olympic sports, as these can easily be found in your home country.

VOLLEYBALL

Beach volleyball courts are hard to come by on weekends, so schedule a few hours in advance on weekdays with **Pele** tel: 9702-5794. R$30 per hour with volleyball and net.

Hang gliding & Paragliding

Your dream of flying is closer than you imagine. By far our highest recommendation, as Rio is one of the few tropical cities in the world where you can hang glide or paraglide over the city and land on a beach. And no, it is not dangerous, (but will kick your adrenaline sky high, no pun).

Regardless of the weather you should call as soon as you arrive and ask to be on stand by, as the favorable wind conditions have little to do with how sunny it is. No training or special gear needed (other than sports-shoes, no sandals), just a shit load of guts.

To fly like a bird you can contact the Sky Center Team (responsible and professional instructors). They offer both hang gliding and paragliding, as well as free transfer to and from your hotel. Safety (they only fly on good wind conditions, so it won't be a short flight) and satisfaction guaranteed.

Sky Center Rio
Contact: Mauricio Monteiro
2437-4592 or 7817-3526
skycenter@skycenter.com.br
www.skycenter.com.br

SPECIAL DEAL FOR OUR READERS CHECK BACK FLAP

Price: Hang or Paraglide = R$240 with free transfer

Scuba Diving - Dive Day

For those of you who are visiting Rio de Janeiro as a tourist or on business, how about enjoying a different sort of leisure?

Warm sunlight, calm and crystalline waters, virgin Atlantic Forest and indescribable natural beauty. This is Angra dos Reis, a paradise only 2 hours from Rio. There are many bays, more than 1,000 beaches and around 365 islands. The largest island is called Ilha Grande, a perfect place for a trip in a boat or a bit of diving.

Arriving in Angra you`ll embark in the Mr. Dunga, a 45 foot trawler with a fully trained crew, and equipped with lifesaving and safety equipment, oxygen, 2 bathrooms, fresh water and a delicious snack service. You`ll then sail around a few of the islands in the Ilha Grande bay, choosing the best places for scuba diving or snorkeling, to enjoy the wonderful clear turquoise waters. Certified divers will have the opportunity to do two dives; and the non-divers can discover the wonders of the submarine world by means of the "baptism" they call Discover Scuba Diving. And for those not wanting so much adventure, they have masks and flippers on board for them to enjoy the peace and beauty of snorkeling, where even from the surface it is possible to see large numbers of multicolored fish, star-fish, turtles and rays.

After the diving you`ll stop for lunch, relax and soak up the wonderful views of Ilha Grande. On the way back, if we have time, you can stop at one of the beaches for a last dive in paradise!

In the evening you`ll return to Rio. Don't miss this chance to visit one of the most beautiful places in Brazil!

Océan Centro de Mergulho
contact: Flávia Fonseca
www.ocean.com.br / info@ocean.com.br
Tel/Fax: 2524-4000 or 7845-0615
Office: R. Alvaro Alvim 24 Gr. 705, Centro
Oper. Base: Enseada do Bananal
Ilha Grande - Angra dos Reis
Prices: R$500 per person, includes car transfer, boat, equipment, lessons, and lunch.

SPECIAL DEAL
FOR OUR READERS
CHECK BACK FLAP

Atlantic Ocean Fishing

Not the cheapest sport, but those who are into it can't miss a chance to catch some in the south seas. Rio is great for marlin fishing, as well as a spectrum of other fish you don't get in the northern hemisphere. Although a pricey sport, it is far cheaper than first world prices.

Most fishing tours include rods, bait, drinks etc, so you just show, sail, fish, drink and eat what you catch before returning.

Marlin Fishing

You'll sail out from Gloria Marina for 2 hours before getting to the sweet spot. Since you are paying by the use of the boat and not the number of people, you can invite your friends and split costs with them.

Marlin Yacht
Contact: Roberto
tel: 9986-9678
marlin@marlinyacht.com.br
www.marlinyacht.com.br

SPECIAL DEAL FOR OUR READERS
CHECK BACK FLAP

From R$1300 for all day fishing trip on 23ft motor boat (fits 7). Includes all equipment. Schedule in advance to be on stand-by for ideal weather and sea conditions.

Bay tour with coastal fishing

Conversely, if you are not professionally into fishing, but would rather play and cruise around, you can opt for the Bay tour, where you can see Rio's coast while tossing the hook in.

From R$700 for all day bay fishing trip on 23ft motor boat (fits 7). Includes all equipment and ice cooler for your drinks.

Island Fishing

Zip over to Cagarra Islands (facing Ipanema beach), where you can snorkel and fish.
From R$500 for 4 hour boat trip

Rock Climbing & Mountanineering

R io is the largest urban rock climbing center in Latin America.

There are many mountains and hills to go for it, specially the two most famous post cards of Rio: Sugar Loaf and Corcovado mountain.

Rock climbing and mountaineering tours are available to everyone moderately fit, even if you never climbed before.

The safety harnesses, ropes and helmets help guarantee you go back home in one piece.

What's more, imagine how cool it would be to make a poster from a picture of you climbing Sugar Loaf or hiking up to the Christ the Redeemer Statue, with the rest of Rio in the background.

Crux Ecoaventura
Contact: Marcelo
Tel: 8734-0581 or 3474-1726
info@cruxecoaventura.com.br
more tours: www.cruxecoaventura.com.br

From R$ 150 pp for a half day climbing tour in Sugar loaf or Corcovado.
R$ 120 pp for a mountaineering tour in Sugar Loaf or Corcovado. This tour has a late version starting at 10am or 11am, for people who party at night. Gear, hotel/tour transfers, trail snacks and guide included.

R$ 120 pp for a half day tour cascading a Botanical Garden Waterfall – rappel down the waterfall on ropes. This tour has a late version starting at 10am or 11am, for people who party at night.

Off Road Biking & Bike Tour

You can do bike tours in Rio City along the Tijuca Forest.

It is outside the mud trails, but you will bike through the city crossing the Atlantic Forest, appreciating panoramic views of Rio de Janeiro, as from Vista Chinesa or the Corcovado hill (Christ Statue).

Those who never went before won't have a hard time keeping up, as most in the groups may be beginners too. Cycle up for 2 hours and then slalom it all back down in a fraction of the time going up.

If you opt for the full day tour, you´ll cycle through Tijuca Forest up to the Christ Statue!

Off – road mountain biking in National and State Parks in Rio is forbidden, so you need to go on a side trip to practice.

One hour from Rio, in the country side of Petrópolis is all hills and mountains, where you can pick up some speed. This is adjusted for the moderately experienced biker.

An ideal sport for cloudy days, even for those "over the hill".

Crux Ecoaventura
Contact: Marcelo
Tel: 8734-0581 or 3474-1726
info@cruxecoaventura.com.br
more tours: www.cruxecoaventura.com.br

Tours range from R$ 120 pp for a half day bike tour in Tijuca Forest to R$ 280 pp for a full day tour in Petrópolis off road districts.

Tijuca Forest tour has a late version starting at 10am or 11am, for people who party at night. Ask for group discounts.

Gear (bike and helmet), hotel/tour transfers, trail snacks and guide included.

Kayaking

R io is all about water. Fresh or salt water.

When you go to the beach, you don't realize how beautiful is seeing the beach from the sea on a sunny day.

Ocean kayaking is an opportunity to get to know the islands of Rio, some of them a preserved environmental area.

With ocean kayaking, you'll be on the warm waters of Rio, facing the beauty of our mountain range and the islands wild life.

You will kayak for a little over an hour exploring Urca and Botafogo bay.

The more experienced kayakers, we offer a tour to the Cagarras islands, the ones right in front of Ipanema beach, demanding more time but the prize will be the exotic wild life present there.

Crux Ecoaventura
Contact: Marcelo
Tel: 8734-0581 or 3474-1726
info@cruxecoaventura.com.br
more tours: www.cruxecoaventura.com.br

Kayak tours starts at R$ 130 pp for the Urca/Botafogo bay tour.
Cagarras islands tour is R$ 180pp.
Ask for group discounts.
Gear (floating suite), hotel/tour transfers, trail snacks and guide included

Wakeboarding and Water Skiing

Wakeboarding has replaced water skiing, just like snowboarding is replacing ski. And with good reason: you have better control of the equipment when you only have to control one rather than two. Although the sea is too bumpy to practice either of these properly, Rio has a lake (Lagoa) that has improved in water quality, while remaining flat year round. Marcos, our recommended instructor for both of these, has two boats, one for wakeboarding (which creates a taller wake), and one for water skiing, which creates as little wake as possible. Ramps and slalom course are installed on the lake.

Rio Wake Center
Contact: Marcos
tel: 9976-7147 or 2239-6976
riowakecenter@riowakecenter.com.br
www.riowakecenter.com.br
Prices: R$165 for an hour of either sport . Time can be split amongst a few people. No experience needed.

SPECIAL DEAL
FOR OUR READERS
CHECK BACK FLAP

Kite Surfing

Kite surfing is the coolest shit! It is the newest water sport and is something you can learn during your stay in Rio. Not only is Rio a great place to practice and learn the sport, but down here lessons are also very affordable compared to 1st World prices (usually about 1/5 of what a similar course runs for out there).

However, it is not for every one. You have to be in shape. If you haven't been working out, you won't be able to keep up with the four-hours-a-day lessons.

They are very demanding. Sort of like working out at the gym for 4 hours.

The fastest way to learn it is to take a 2-day class. The first day you learn how to fly the kite and then to body-drag, which is to lay in the water and control the kite so it drags you around. The next day you learn to stand up on the board, and possibly do a few manoevers and jumps.

The best places in Rio to learn to kite surf is Barra beach, around the posto 2 and 3. It offers steady wind conditions (5 days a week average), warm waters for you to learn, waves and lots of space.

CWS KiteSurfing Lessons
Contact: Carlito
Tel: 8606-7497
www.riocharm.com
2 Day course (3-4 hours on each day), starting at R$720

SPECIAL DEAL
FOR OUR READERS
CHECK BACK FLAP

Surfing

Surfing is still the coolest beach sport. Just mentioning it impresses ladies anywhere in the world. But learning it is hard, exhausting, and takes many days. From the two hours you spend in the water, over 60 minutes are spent swimming on the board. The other 55 are spent waiting for a wave, and the last 2 minutes is the time you spend riding the wave. (Really, no shit).

Unless you are staying more than a week in Rio, we don't recommend taking the classes as they will take up 2 hours a day and wear you out for the rest of the day. Unless you are in Olympic conditions, you won't be able to take more than 2 hours a day. Most students are only able to stand on the board on the second day, and it takes about 7 lessons before you are doing basic manoevers. But, if you have started taking lessons elsewhere, feel confident about your physical condition and want to try it anyway, we recommend this world famous instructor:

Rico de Souza Surf School
Contact: Rico or Andreia
Barra beach at posto 5
Tel: 2438-1692 or 8817-7190 or 2438-4096
Prices: R$50 per person per hour of individual lessons or R$40 pp per hour in group of 3.

Bodyboarding

A safer alternative to learning to surf is to body board. It is much easier to learn (you pick up the basic moves in under an hour), less tiring, and you ride the waves longer. All these are arguments in favor of this sport. It loses to surfing only in that surfing carries a status. At the same time, many argue that body boarding is a radical version of surf, while safer.

Riding a wave on a body board is idiotically simple, but instructors can teach you the cool stuff: back flips, rolls, 360 and an endless sea of tribal jargon. Plus, you learn to ride big waves at high speeds. We recommend taking bodysurfing classes with this instructor:

Kung Body Board School
Contact: Marcos Kung
Tel: 9442-3335 or 3411-2128

calkung@hotmail.com
www.kungbodyboards.com.br
Barra beach outpost 4 1/2 (in front of Av.Sernambetiba 3360)

Prices: 2 hour of private body boarding lessons =R$100 : 24 hour scheduling

Baroque wrought-iron work on front door of the São Bento monas

CULTURAL

THE 90 SECOND HISTORY OF BRAZIL

For those of you who haven't done your research, here goes:

Brazilian history is closely parallel to that of the US: It was discovered in 1500 and soon colonized by the Portuguese.

First, brazil-wood was extracted for its red pigment. By 1600 the Portuguese were trying to cultivate the land with slave labor.

The natives wouldn't be enslaved, so most were hunted and killed. African slaves were brought to Rio and Bahia to help with the cultivation of new plants, mostly coffee, cotton, tobacco, sugar and cocoa.

In the 1700s a gold rush broke out in Minas Gerais. Most of the gold and precious stones were extracted (under strict supervision by the Portuguese crown) and sent to Europe for trading.

The locals didn't like the idea of not seeing the profits, so they started plotting independence from Portugal.

The capital of Brazil was moved from Salvador to Rio (not because of the night life).

In the middle of the 19th century, the British abolished slavery and forced other emerging economies to do the same, so no one would have a competitive advantage. Brazil followed suit and abolished slavery.

In the meantime, Brazil became a republic after the king of Portugal lost his throne to democracy.

In the 20th century, there was a massive influx of Germans, Italians and Japanese, which helped organize the place a bit.

Brazil was never in any major war, mostly because Brazilians don't really want to live anywhere else in the world.

Luckily, it was never attacked by anyone, except the French and the Dutch, who kept trying to invade, but where repeatedly defeated.

Cultural Downtown

Although Rio has a lot of history and cultural attractions, we have narrowed down our recommendations to include only the essentials, doable in a 2 day tour of the center. Est.Total Time (T): 5h per day Est. Total Cost (C): R$ 80 Best on: Cloudy/Rainy Day

As far as museums, churches and historic areas, our recommendations are to spend a day or two visiting as many of the following as quickly as possible (1 hour visits):

Day 1

❶ MODERN ART MUSEUM

The MAM is itself a work of modern art by one of Brazil's greatest architects Eduardo Affonso Reidy, also responsible for the Flamengo park project (together with Burle Marx).

❷ MOSTEIRO DE SÃO BENTO

A rich monastery with one of the most ornate baroque style churches in Latin America, with tons of gold work.

LUNCH

Esch Cafe: Rua do Rosario 107
Delirio Tropical: Rua da Assembleia 36

❸ CENTRO CULTURAL BANCO DO BRASIL

Always has some technological exhibit. Very nice space.

❹ PAÇO IMPERIAL

The imperial home, now transformed into an art museum

Day 2

❺ SELARON STAIRS

Selaron, one of the most original artists on the scene for the last 20 years, paints pregnant favela cartoon women on tiles. This 80m staircase with tiles from all over the world is a true work of art (a collection of works of art), and he is always there in the mornings, painting.

❻ CATEDRAL

Another one of Reidy's works. Although massive looking from the outside, it has very powerful lighting and sound effects inside.

7 BIBLIOTECA NACIONAL

One of the largest libraries in the world, with over 4 million works.

8 TEATRO MUNICIPAL

Beautiful classical building, with an excess of imported marble.

HAPPY-HOURS:
Arco do Teles, Centro
Mercado 32, Rua Mercado 32
Carioca Da Gema, Lapa

For a personalized tour of Rio's culture, Maria Yolen's Rio Custom Tours is recommended. Maria is an excellent guide who likes to show more than just the postcard views. Sunday mass at Sao Bento, complete with Gregorian chants, and a tour through Santa Teresa are the most popular. She will pick you up and drop you off at your hotel.

Rio Charm Tours
8606-7497
www.riocharm.com
info@riocharm.com
Call for prices on custom tours

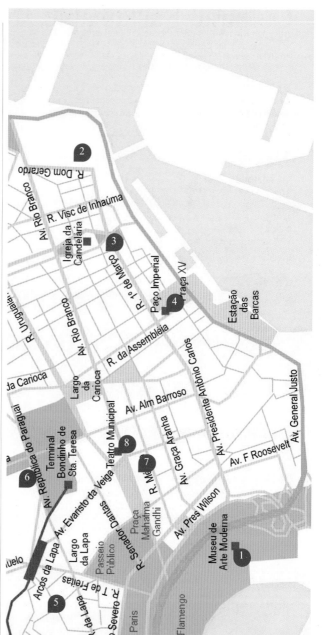

Cultural: Sustainable Tour of Favela

One of the most successful and requested tours. A walking tour through the alleys, visiting the local handicraft, arts, schools and local commerce. A must for everyone.

Est. Total Time: 3h Est. Total Cost: R$ 65   Best on: sunny or cloudy days

Rejane Reis, owner of Exotic Tours, has been doing sustainable work in the favelas since 1998, where she trains local people how to be guides. In this Tourism Workshop they learn English, Spanish, tourism and get to know the touristic points of Rio. The locals that guide you on this tour were able to improve with Rejane's help to become professionals guides, working also outside the favela.

If you are looking for an insider point of Brazilian view, the favela tourism will introduce you to another Rio.

Exotic Tours
Contact: Rejane Reis
tel: 7827-3024
Local Toll Free: 0800 282 6972
rejanereis@exotictours.com.br
www.exotictours.com.br
Price: R$65 pp = 3 hour tour with transfer included.
Everyday at 2:00pm
Also available: Samba School Rehearsal

Cultural: Tree-hugger Tour

If you have never been in an Atlantic forest before, this is it. It is best carried out with guides, but can be done alone if you have a car, map and guts.

Est. Total Time (T): 5h Est. Total Cost (C): R$ 70   Best on: partially cloudy weekdays

PEDRA BONITA AT TIJUCA NATIONAL FOREST

You will start off with a light hike up to the top of Pedra Bonita, one of Rio's nicest views. There you will enjoy a view of Rio few people have had the privilege to see, and watch the hang-gliders and para-gliders jumping off the ramp.

SANTA TERESA

You will then proceed by car to St. Teresa, to visit this cute colonial neighborhood, riding the trolley to Largo do Guimaraes, stopping for lunch.

CORCOVADO

After lunch, you have two options: Option 1) you can visit the Tijuca forest, a completely

reforested area of Rio. There you will get to see all kinds of vegetation, some wildlife, and a waterfall.

Option 2) ride up to Corcovado and visit the Christ statue.

Brazil Expedition
Contact: Eduardo tel: 9998-2907
www.brazilexpedition.com
tours@brazilexpedition.com
Price: from R$75)= Monday to
Saturday. Includes hotel pick-up and
entrance to Christ Statue.

GIVING

My Chicago buddy passed a beggar on the street and handed him a R$50 note before I could stop him. When asked why, he replied that he was grateful for what God had given him and wanted to give back.

Unfortunately, the beggars and "injured mothers" sitting in Ipanema are predators of your weakness: they pay as much as R$2000 rent to the local mafia to be able to sit outside an international bank and beg. Some women rent babies, give them sleeping pills and beg at the rate of R$120 a day.

So for those of you wanting to give something back to those in need, we have done some due diligence and selected 4 charities that are making a change and setting an example to others in third world countries.

Most of these are not structured to accept web payments such as Paypal or credit cards, but all have a website with methods of donation, or you can also visit them personally to donate, giving you a chance to understand how it will be used. The charity workers will be more than pleased to show you around. And any amount is welcome.

ORPHAN KIDS: FAMÍLIA SANTA CLARA

Even though Cicero and Eliete are married and have 3 children it was not enough. They decided to follow their dream and make an effective contribution to society, so they created the "Família Santa Clara".

The family embraces 70 children who are at social risk. Many have been abandoned by their natural parents, and many are orphans abandoned by society. The Familia Santa Clara works as a real substitute to traditional institutions and orphanages, whereby it offers the invaluable opportunity of a life with a family.

Their mission is to offer a family, education and culture to the children they embrace, preparing them for life, up to the point when they are ready to build their own families and start a life of their own, re-integrated into society.

With over 18 years of dedication and hard work, the Familia Santa Clara has been widely recognized and praised by Unesco, IDB (Inter-american Development Bank), and FIA (Foundation for the Infants and Adolescents of Rio de Janeiro) for it's social importance, giving children an opportunity to be children, in a place where love and respect are primary rules.

If you want to help, check their site with a presentation in English
www.familiasantaclara.org.br

STREET KIDS: PROJETO UERÊ

Projeto Uerê is a non-profit organization working with children and youth at risk in the streets and in very poor communities in Rio de Janeiro, Brazil.

BACK

Children and youth living on the streets have self-destructive behavior and are at high risk from diseases like HIV, drug addiction and violence. In Brazil there are at least 23 million youngsters nationwide that live under similar conditions.

The work Uerê offers inside these poor communities is of a preventive nature due to interpersonal and intergroup conflicts. Rio has narcotic dealers that keep the poor population under their "protection" which turns the work very difficult and dangerous.

Projeto Uerê contributes towards improving life quality of some of those children synthesized in a school that provides special education as well as a day-care center adapted to the very special needs of the kids it cares for.

They work with a methodology specific for each child and for the difficulties the children have in learning.

To learn more about how you can help them:
www.projetouere.org.br/eng/

You can Help: Iko Poran

If you really want to help, you can donate sweat instead of money. You can join Iko Poran and become a volunteer, staying a few weeks to a few months in Brazil and putting your back into helping any of the various NGOs associated with Iko Poran.

Iko Poran Association has as its purpose the fight against many forms of social exclusion. It organizes national and international volunteers, of various areas, especially ecology, education, health, artistic, cultural, sciences. They promote the social assistance directly or indirectly to infants, teens, and to socially excluded communities, caring for the

rescue of their citizenship and social reintegration.

Acting as a volunteer you also develop a totally new perspective of the world and commit yourself with the social responsibility that can turn the Earth sustainable for all its inhabitants.
www.ikoporan.org

Amazon: PreserveAmazonia

As we all know, the Amazon is the world's largest forest, serving as an air filter and temperature balancer to the Earth. Meanwhile, it is shrinking at an ever growing pace, and the only way to stop it is through awareness and education.

That's where Preserve Amazonia comes in, offering viable alternatives to the local's needs and bringing attention to the actions of its antagonists. Further, they help create awareness of it both politically and in the media.
www.preserveamazonia.com

Silly Pastimes

SKOL TIME

Down here to party all week with your buddies? Draw a watch on your wrist, pointing the hour hand to a "Skol" marker, and leave your real watch at home. Whenever your buddies ask what time it is, it will be "Skol Time", and you all have to chug one.

FOLLOW HOT-CHICK

Not stalking, just anthropology... and it's the funniest shit. Hang around Padaria Ipanema on Rua Visconde de Piraja with Rua Joana Angelica during the day waiting for a foxy woman to pass by. Follow her, staying 10 steps behind. Now watch everyone's reaction as she passes: eyes will open, jaw's will drop, cars will stop, drool will splatter and necks will crack out loud, turning to get a complete evaluation.

MID-NIGHT SOCCER GAME AT FLAMENGO

There are freaks playing soccer till 5 in the morning at the soccer fields in Flamengo. And they serve beer and barbecue! The famous "amateur league" games to watch for are the Doorman team against the Waiters. To get there, ask your taxi driver "Campo de futebol no Aterro do Flamengo"

BEER UNDER BAT TREE

In to Batman? Who isn't. If you are hardcore, you're into bats too. How about a beer under the BatTree, in Praça Nossa Senhora da Paz in Ipanema? Walking around the park you'll see bats on a tree like electrons to a proton. They usually don't bite, but that's how the adrenaline will kick in.

GETTING DRUNK ON THE PADDLE BOATS

They got these super-cheesy paddle boats on the Lagoa during November to December at night (during the day all year round). But if you bring a bottle of champagne, vodka or wine, the cheesiness will melt away, specially if accompanied by a cigar or what not.

Taxi instruction "Pedalinho da Lagoa, na reta do Corte de Cantagalo".

Afterwards head over to Palaphita Kitsch, the Amazonian kiosk 100 ft away.

VISIT SELARON

Not silly, but definitely a pastime. Selaron is already mentioned in the Cultural tour, but his work is so cool it is worth emphasizing. Get to Lapa and ask for "Escadaria Selaron". Once there, chill with him. Mornings only.

Emergencies

A visit to Rio is no trip do Disney World. It is a big city, with its fair share of problems. Should you get into an emergency situation, be sure to follow these procedures to bring things back to normal.

ILL OR INJURED

Although Rio has somewhat of a free medical assistance offered by the state, most 1st world visitors may not like the response time Brazilians have become accustomed to.

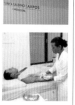

Long waiting lines and lack of English speaking attendants may worsen your medical problem.

Luckily there is a clinic devoted to working with tourists 24 hours a day, and in several languages (English, Spanish and French).

They have the necessary infrastructure, or partnerships with other clinics, to cure what ails you, from simple colds to minor surgery.

Should you need to, they can also visit you at your hotel. What's more, they work with most international health plans and traveller's insurance.

Galdino Campos Clinic
Contact: Ronaldo Galdino Campos
Rua NS Copacabana 492
Tel:2548-9966
www.galdinocampos.com.br
Member of the International Society of
Travel Medicine

ROBBED

First say your prayers if you weren't physically assaulted or attacked. Second, hop over to the Tourist Police Station in Leblon (Av. Afranio de Melo 159 or call 3399-7170). They may not be able to recoup your belongings, but can issue a police report for insurance purposes, and issue an alert to patrol cars to better serve that area.

ARRESTED

Were you a bad boy (or girl)? Or were you set up by "the man"? In either case, nothing like a slick lawyer to squeeze you out. To find a best one for your needs, contact your consulate, listed in the back cover.

LOST PASSPORT

Should you lose your passport (it shouldn't have left the hotel in the first place), be sure to contact your consulate as they can produce a quick fix. Check the back cover for a list of local consulates and numbers.

LOST FLIGHT

Over slept? Unless you are here during extreme high season, you may be able to extend your stay for US$75 or so. Check the list at the back for the local office for major airlines.

STOMACH ACHE

You ate the peppers, right? Or was it the street caipirinhas with questionable ice? We bad mouth it so much people get curious about them... oh well. What my buddy, who was travelling through India, used to do whenever he got the runs would be to mix a finger of vinegar with a finger of water and gulp it down. That would kill whatever was wrecking havoc in his stomach. He would later drink some yogurt to bring his intestinal flora back up. Soon he would drink a few coconut waters (agua de coco) to hydradte. Has worked for him and others, but surely this is something I can't recommend because I'm not a doctor.... just a trick I heard...

RIP OFFS

Should you get tricked by any establishment in Rio, whether a tampered taxi or a restaurant waiter or a bait&switch shop, contact me. The only things that boils my blood is poor customer service and paying for dumb movies. I live for this, and will try to use all my super-powers to put them in their place.
cris@rioforpartiers.com

Remember to keep the Emergency Contacts Card (see back cover) always in your pocket.

RAINY DAY OPTIONS

WHAT TO DO IN RIO

SHOP

Heck, you are bound to find a lot of the same international shops at the local malls (Levi's, Armani, etc.) but some shops offer stuff at good prices you can't find elsewhere: Brazilian pants for women, shoes and bags, beach gear.
Check page 82 for gift ideas

FRUIT TASTING AT THE PRODUCE FAIR

There is one going on every day, so why not spend an hour trying all the tropical fruits available?
Check page 155 for daily schedule

CAPOEIRA LESSON

Capoeira is an African-Brazilian martial art/dance developed by slaves for their defense as well as their mental and physical balance. It works every muscle in your body. Its practice has grown internationally in the last few years, and you can get a taste for it in a lesson or two with master Nestor in his academy. Single lessons (2 hours) are available at 7pm every day of the week for R$30 each.
Centro Cultural Casa Rosa
contact: Rodrigo
8877-8804 or 2557-2562
Rua Alice 550, Laranjeiras
R$50 per person, minimum 2. Call by 11am for afternoon private lessons. Or show up on tuesdays and thursdays at 7pm and join the on-going group R$30

SCUBA LESSONS

Hey! It is raining! Why not get wet! Go get some scuba diving lessons! Check page 57 for details.

MASSAGE PARLOR
See page 85 for options

MUSEUMS

The museums listed on page 68 may offer enough content to last a few hours without boring you to death.

WHEN IT'S RAINING

DANCE LESSONS

You can either sit around waiting for the sun to come out, or you can go learn a few dance moves! Really! Just call and schedule private lessons (individual or group). Dance lessons last 2 hours, and should be enough to last a lifetime of showing off.

Your options of dance lessons are: Samba (Samba de Pe), Ballroom samba, Zouk (a new, more sensual Lambada) and Forro.
Centro Cultural Casa Rosa
contact: Rodrigo
8877-8804 or 2557-2562
Rua Alice 550, Laranjeiras
R$50 per person, minimum 2. Call by 11am for afternoon private lessons. Or show up on tuesdays and thursdays at 7pm and join the on-going group R$30

BRAZILIAN COOKING CLASSES

Like to cook? Want to play around and learn some Brazilian recipes to show to your friends back home? You can take some cooking classes, learn it all, and of course, eat it all.

Cook Rio offers cooking lessons to small groups, starting at 7pm, eating by 9pm. Call by 2pm to schedule and choose from:

A) *Feijoada* menu: *caipinha*, pork rinds, *feijoada* (meat&beans stew, rice, collard greens, oranges, *farofa*, rice), banana sweet for dessert.

B) Shrimp *Muqueca* (Bahian) menu: *Batida de coco* drink, shrimp *Muqueca* with rice and *farofa*, *Manjar* for dessert.

C) Kid's menu: *brigadeiro*, carrot cake with chocolate topping and colored chicken skewers.

These lessons only include ingredients that can be readily found in the US or EU countries.
Cook Rio
Contact: Bryan tel: 8606-7497
info@cookrio.com www.cookrio.com
Lessons start at R$120 per person and should be scheduled as soon as you arrive, or with 24hrs notice. SPECIAL DEAL FOR OUR READERS CHECK BACK FLAP

THE TASTY IPANEMA

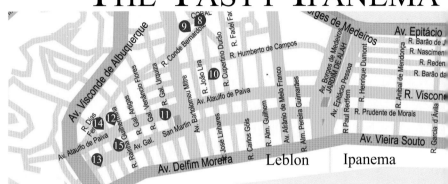

The oldest man in the world says his secret to longevity is to walk around the block and have a beer every day. So this crawl should make you immortal.

Of course you don't want to go it alone or with just one friend, as that can get boring or repetitive. So my proposal is for everyone doing a crawl around Ipanema and Leblon to be at the established times and places mentioned here, so you can make new friends and have fresh conversations. Or you can hire my services, which don't cost anything, just my expenses.

Don't have breakfast or lunch before starting. This pub-crawl route is designed to get you to discover Ipanema and Leblon's bars, taste all the popular Brazilian bar foods and snacks, and of course, to get hammered. An average of 2 beers and 45 minutes per bar is a good pace to keep. Also, before leaving, write your hotel's name and room in a card. Keep it in your pocket.

⓪ PHARMACY

Go to any pharmacy (*farmacia*) and ask for 4 ENGOVs per person in your group, a hang-over deterrent. Take two each.

❶ BRASILEIRINHO AT 1PM

Brasileirinho, on Rua Jangadeiros on Praça General Osorio Square is the east most bar in Ipanema. Order a *chopp* and a "*caldinho de feijão*" (check page 149). If you are in to fresh fried pork rinds (real men are), ask for "*torresmo*".

❷ BELMONTE

Belmonte's winner snack is the shrimp *pastel* ("*pastel de camarão*"), where they manage to stuff it with 13 shrimps. So order this. Their other prized item is the *empada de camarão* (shrimp cup-cake). If you're not into shrimp, ask for jerked beef (carne seca). Their Brahma *chopp* is top notch.

❸ MANUEL & JOAQUIM

"Bolinho de bacalhau", cod cake balls, is their specialty.

❹ SINDICATO DO CHOPP

"Isca de file" (steak strips) is not bad, however large.

❺ DEVASSA 3:30PM

Rio's premium micro-brew. First ask for the *loira*, then the *ruiva*, then the *negra*. Repeat if in love. Their "porção de pastel" (portion of turn-overs) in their various flavours is also gourmet.

❻ GAROTA DE IPANEMA

The chopp is great, and their portion of "kibe" stands out from the rest.

❼ INFORMAL 6PM

The most formal of *botequims* (brazilian pubs), has great Brahma beer, while their "bolinho de aipim com carne moida" (beef cassava cake) is

LEBLON PUB CRAWL

scrumptious. A trip to their cold cuts and appetizer table is worth it, as you can choose what you want and pay by the weight.

Completing this, and if still bubbly and not drunk, get in a cab and head to your next destination, Leblon.

8 DESACATO 7PM

Cab to the beginning of Rua Conde Bernadote. Their angle is kick-ass shish-kababs at rock bottom prices, so order 2 "espetinhos" per person and share.

9 ACADEMIA DA CACHAÇA

"Linguica acebolada" (onion with fried sausage).

10 BRACARENSE 9PM

"Bolinho de bacalhau", yes, again, as it is Rio's best.

11 CONVERSA FIADA

"Casquinha de siri" (shredded crab in a shell).

12 JOBI

Considered one of Rio's top chopp. They are also good at a lot of finger foods, but "carne seca com aipim frito" (fried cassava with jerked beef) is a must.

13 DEVASSA 11PM

Just like spot #5, so good worth a second visit.

14 PIZZARIA GUANABARA

Rio's end of the night stop for those not getting some. Extra cheesy pizza is worth checking out.

15 ENGOV AND COCONUT

Engov only works if you take it again at the end, so take two or three. Now chug a coconut water or two.

By now you should be pretty plastered. So rent a car, get full insurance, and drive till the air bags go off. Or get in a cab and give him the hotel card.

Caipirinha Crawl

Of course, this pub crawl could be replaced with caipirinhas. One per pub, and if you make it past Bracarense, call a coroner.

Cachaças to ask for: Magnifica, Salinas, Ferreira, Meia Lua, Boazinha, Vendaval, Germana.

Fruits to ask for are:

Lime- *Limão* (regular)

Lemon-*Lima*

Pineapple - *Abacaxi*

Strawberry- *Morango*

Passion Fruit - *Maracujá*

Lychee- *Lichia*

SHOP: GIFT IDEAS

There is no trick to shopping other than knowing where to go and what to get, so here are our suggestions for gift ideas and stores that are well-kept secrets. These are a must for those into import-export.

BRASIL E CIA POPULAR ART

Do not miss it! They have all the Brazilian popular art objects made of ceramics, fiber, wood, paper, textile or even gourd! The best selection of perfect gifts ideas. Cute pieces, easy to carry back home, that will tell a little bit of Brazilian history, and delight parts of your home. Robust packaging available for delicate pieces.

Brasil e Cia

SPECIAL DEAL FOR OUR READERS CHECK BACK FLAP

www.brasilecia.com.br
Rua Maria Quitéria 27, Ipanema
2267-4603

VIVARA

Tired of cheesy baroque jewelry? Looking for elegant and whimsical pieces that will get everyone´s attention? Check out Vivara's designer line-up of rings, bracelets, necklaces and ear-rings.

Vivara
Rio Sul Mall, Botafogo
Shopping Leblon, Leblon
Barra Shopping Mall
Botafogo Praia Shopping Mall
www.vivara.com.br
0800 726 2000

Brazilian Music CDs

Bar do Mineiro, for bar chilling. Djavan CD, great for love making. Tom Jobim for after sex music. Found at: Modern Sound and other music stores.

Cuban and Brazilian Cigars

Cuban cigars are legal here, and very cheap (US$25 for a Cohiba, US$15 for Patargas) To bring them back through customs, just take the ring off.
Esch Cafe (Casa del Habano)
Rua Dias Ferreira 78, Leblon
Rua do Rosario 107, Centro

OTHER GIFT IDEAS

Coffee-table books on Brazil

Brazilian soccer team shirt.

Cachaça Bottle

& HIDDEN TREASURES

When window shopping, you will notice things like "4X" preceding the price, meaning that the actual price is 4 times the number following it. This is because most stores will lay-away, even cheap stuff like shoes or books.

GILSON MARTINS

For 20 Years Gilson has been at it: designing hand bags and accessories. After winning dozens of fashion and design competitions, he opened his store, featuring his creations. His stuff is really good, and bring lots of credit cards, as you`ll want to max them out, and get all his products.

Gilson Martins
Rua Visconde de Pirajá 146, Ipanema
Rua Fiqueiredo Magalhães 304, Copa
Rio Sul Mall, store 116 2nd Floor
www.gilsonmartins.com.br

SPECIAL DEAL
FOR OUR READERS
CHECK BACK FLAP

GAROTA DE IPANEMA SHOP

Named after the famous Girl from Ipanema, this store will make you look your best at the beach. They have all kinds of shapes, sizes and patterns of bathing suits and shorts. The Brazilian theme shirts are a good way to take a piece of Rio home. The atmosphere is very welcoming, and Ipanema's trendy charm and sensuality is all over the place.

Loja Garota de Ipanema
www.garotadeipanemabrasil.com.br
Rua Vinicius de Moraes 53, Ipanema
2521-3168

SPECIAL DEAL
FOR OUR READERS
CHECK BACK FLAP

PÉ DE BOI

One of the most complete popular art stores in all of Brazil: so interesting it could double as a folklore museum, and hence further reason for a visit. Ana Maria, the owner, travels around Brazil visiting famous local artists looking for unique hand crafted pieces with interesting background stories, guaranteeing them to be the icing on your living room. International shipping available for larger pieces.

Pé de Boi
Rua Ipiranga 55, Laranjeiras
2285-4395
www.pedeboi.com.br

SPECIAL DEAL
FOR OUR READERS
CHECK BACK FLAP

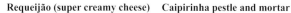

| Doce de leite can | Requeijão (super creamy cheese) | Caipirinha pestle and mortar |

SPOILED-ROTTEN GIRLY

Weather cloudy or rainy? Use and abuse the various beauty services available in Rio.

DERMATOLOGY

Aestheticians and dermatologists in Rio are ready to make you look your best. Given the highly competitive beauty war between Carioca women, the professionals have no choice but to stay ahead with the latest techniques and technologies in skin rejuvenation.

Diode Laser for epilation, Botox, CoolTouch, Pixel, IPL device for skin spots and spider veins, Thermage for contouring, fillers and peels or a good old fashion facial are the most requested by tourists, since you can walk in and out in under 2 hours. To know all your options, schedule an appointment. A wise option for rainy days.

AmaDerm
Contact: Luciana
Rua Visconde de Piraja 433 - 5th floor
Ipanema
tel: 2287-9696
luciana@amaderm.com.br
www.amaderm.com.br

HAIR DRESSER

Edward Scissor hands ain't got shit on Hans. "He knows how to make a better you" is the saying in Ipanema. This is an ideal option after all the damage the sun has done to your hair. Styling and moisturizing is all it needs so you can go back home looking your best.

They have other services available too: Brazil is one of the few places where girls get rid of the cuticles, making your nails prettier and cleaner. The "Misturinha", very popular in Rio, is a mixture of pale color nail polish.

Also: Wonder why Brazilians wear small bikinis? Brazilian wax! The world known system is a day to remember, do it as soon as you get in Rio, your days at the beach will be much easier!

Hans Coiffeur
Contact: Claudia
Rua Visconde de Piraja 646, Ipanema
tel: 2259-7654 or 2294-5155
www.hanscoiffeur.com.br

DENTIST

Ok, maybe not just for girls. Like other beauty services, lots of 1st worlders come to Brazil and improve their smile: whitening, ceramic crowns, laminates and whatever can be carried out in a few hours and some don't need a 2nd checkup. The US$300 you can save on teeth whitening or cap replacements can help pay for you ticket here.

Multi Oral's clients are mostly the American and English community in Rio, as well as tourists. They have English speaking dentists as well as French. To get started, email them telling them what date you'll be arriving, what services you want rendered and when you'll be leaving. They'll email back with a time and place, prices and a request for confirmation. Once in Rio, cab over to their offices in Ipanema.

Multi Oral
Contact: Esther Klein
Rua Visconde de Piraja 433 - 6th floor
Ipanema
2247-0236

SPECIAL DEAL
FOR OUR READERS
CHECK BACK FLAP

contato@multioral.com.br
www.multioral.com.br

PAMPERING OPTIONS

MASSAGE

What's better than sex? That's right: massages. And since you are here, why not go big? At the Urban Spa Maria Bonita, you choose from 5 kind of massages:

- Ayurvedic
- Relaxing
- Shirodhara
- Swedish
- Shiatsu

Therapies:

- Colon Therapy
- Hot Stones

The perfect stop after the beach considering it`s right behind Posto 9.

Maria Bonita Urban Spa
Contact: Tadeu
Rua Prudente de Morais 729
2513-4050
spa@spamariabonita.com.br
www.spamariabonita.com.br
Roughly R$120 for 1 hour with up to 3 types of massages.

COSMETIC SURGERY

Beautiful beaches, beautiful bodies, the two go hand in hand. As such, it should be no surprise that Brazil has long been the beautification destination of Hollywood celebrities and, more recently, of savvy world travelers.

Helping tourists interested in combining their getaway with elective plastic surgery, CosmeticVacations is a U.S. corporation based in Rio de Janeiro that specializes in arranging HIGH quality plastic surgery services for travelers.

Their multi-lingual staff assists tourist patients throughout their stay and is dedicated to connecting clients, whose top priorities are quality and safety, with their highly credentialed partner surgeons and cosmetic surgery clinics. These surgeons offer all types of cosmetic procedures, from the most highly specialized traditional surgeries to the latest procedures with enhanced results.

CosmeticVacations will help plan the trip, including flights and accommodation, as well as provide an array of pre and post-operative activities – all for 30-50% less than comparable surgeons and services in the US and Europe, without sacrificing quality standards.

Constantly monitoring the results of their surgeons to ensure the greatest possible customer satisfaction, CosmeticVacations is committed to keeping the world capital of plastic and cosmetic surgery home to quality and safe procedures for foreigners.

CosmeticVacations
Contact: Michael Boeckle
US Toll free: 1-877-627-2556
(305) 433-8377
(212) 537-6562
Rio (55 21) 2524-8184
info@cosmeticvacations.com
www.CosmeticVacations.com

Free samba jam session on Thursdays and Fridays at Kamikase on Rua do Mercado, Centro

SOUNDS FROM BRAZIL

Live music in Rio Scenarium

SAMBA

The most famous Brazilian music, mostly of percussion and ukelete guitars. Very hard to stay still to. Ask someone to teach you the dance moves, as they seem hard, but are even harder when you try it. Can be heard at any of the samba club rehearsals. Goes great with beer or more hyper stuff.

CDs AND BANDS TO LOOK FOR:

Sambas De Enredo Carnaval De 2007

Cartola

Jamelão

Casa De Samba (Coletânea)

WHERE TO HEAR IT LIVE:

Salgueiro Tue and Sat

Mangueira Wed and Sat

Severyna on Thursdays

Lapa (various spots)

LESSONS

For samba drumming lessons, contact:

Centro Cultural Casa Rosa
contact: Rodrigo
8877-8804 or 2557-2562
Rua Alice 550, Laranjeiras

PAGODE

An improvised samba, made by beating anything that can be found at a bar table: spoon to a bottle as the cymbal, a chair as the drum, matchbox as the shaker etc. Dirty lyrics. Usually women start to dance along to it. Great for afternoons and barbecues.

CDs AND BANDS TO LOOK FOR:

Jorge Aragão

Zeca Pagodinho

Fundo De Quintal

Beth Carvalho

WHERE TO HEAR IT LIVE:

Clementina

Bip Bip

Rua do Mercado on Fridays

CHORINHO

A more vocal and slower version of samba, with fewer beats, making it more melancholic. It emerged in the 19th Century and remains to this day. Not for daily consumption, as its pace can mellow out the excitable.

CDs AND BANDS TO LOOK FOR:

Pixinguinha

Jacob Do Bandolin

Joel Nascimento

WHERE TO HEAR IT LIVE:

Praia Vermelha on Mon,Wed,Fri

Centro Cultural Carioca

Rio Scenarium

Bar do Ze

FUNK

Nothing like American funk, but basically a retard on an electronic piano playing "music" after only one lesson. Mix that with dirty lyrics and what do you get? The biggest music craze in Brazil since the Lambada. Girls love dancing to it, guys love singing the naughty lyrics, parents hate it, in other words, just the way teenage music should be.

Some of the most famous are "I'll throw you on the bed and give lots of pressure" and "the horsy and the donkey took my mare for a walk, clopty clop, clopty clop, clopty clop". Regardless of whether the music makes your ears bleed, the women that listen to this are 90% *poposudas*, meaning, worth the sacrifice.

CDs AND BANDS TO LOOK FOR:

Mr Catra

Dj Marlboro

Cindinho E Doca

WHERE TO HEAR IT LIVE:

Via Show

Parties in Favelas

Some spots in Lapa

Brazilian Pop (MPB)

Caetano, Gil, Marisa Monte, Djavan and Jorge Benjor, amongst many others, used to play in the 60s and 70s a smooth and an upbeat Brazilian version of pop. Unfortunately, most of them offer poetic lyrics that don't mean anything when translated, making its enjoyment hard. But the instrumentals, melodies and voices are vary pleasant to the ear. Get a Jorge Benjor for your car, Djavan for your sofa, Gil for your garden and Marisa Monte for your bed. If you make a Brazilian friend who is willing to translate, get Chico Buarque, and get ready for a major head-rush.

CDs and Bands to look for:
Gilberto Gil
Jorge Benjor
Caetano Veloso
Djavan

Where to hear it live:
Copacabana beach on Sundays
Canecão
Fundição Progresso
Severyna on Fridays

Bossa Nova

Bossa Nova is the grandfather of lounge music, that tranquil sound you hear when you think of casinos in the 50's, Frank Sinatra and ocean views. Tom Jobim (Antonio Carlos Jobim), is the Picasso of this music genre and, many believe, did more to put Brazil on the international music scene than any other individual. Today it is still enjoyed by mature listeners, and everyone else in the boudoir scene. Ideal for before and after sex music.

CDs and Bands to look for:
Tom Jobim
Vinicius de Morais
João Gilberto

Where to hear it live:
Mistura Fina
Esch Cafe
Vinicius Piano Bar
Modern Sound

Forró

Forró music is a slowed-down version of a barn dance: very country. It was so out of style that it came back and is popular again. Basically, you grab a girl (a great reason to grab women) and dance like everyone else in the room: real close rotating clockwise. Two steps out, two steps in, then the other foot. Repeat all night.

CDs and Bands to look for:

Luis Gonzaga

Dominginhos

Jackson Do Pandeiro

Where to hear it live:

Severyna on Mondays

Rio Scenarium

Feira de São Cristovão

Rock

If rock lyrics vaguely make sense in English, then in Portuguese they are just as impenetrable. And given the music industry's woes, talented new artists have not emerged in a while. What the boys and girls have been doing is reviving the bands from the 70's, like the Mutantes, Raul Seixas (Brazil's answer to Bob Dylan, but on even more drugs), Secos e Molhados and others, all of which still have a very fresh sound. (Rumor has it that Kurt Cobain gave a CD of the Mutantes to Beck back in 94 and told him to analyze their style.)

CDs and Bands to look for:

Rita Lee

Casia Eller

Cidade Negra

Mutantes

Where to hear it live:

Canecão

Circo Voador

Fundição Progresso

Electronic

Drum&Bass is finally picking up, and Brazil already has 2 internationally-recognized heroes: DJ Marky and DJ Patife. Both  do random gigs at Bunker, so check the flyers. Chico Science also did a lot as far as helping Brazil define its unique electronic sound while influencing international artists.

CDs and Bands to look for:

Clara Morena

Dj. Patife

Bossa Cuca Nova

Where to hear it live:

Bunker

Rave Parties

YEARLY

JANUARY

VACATION MONTH

January is vacation month for schools and government offices, so everyone is partying it up day and night. Most of the upper class won't be in Rio this month, but can be found in Buzios, Ilha Grande and Paraty, as well as other parts of Brazil. The samba club rehearsals are heating up, so attend as many as you can.

20TH OF JANUARY

Saint Sebastian Day: Only In Rio

CARNIVAL SCHEDULE

To get the most up-to-date info on the carnival parties, visit our site at
www.rioforpartiers.com/samba.html

FEBRUARY

CARNIVAL

Carnival is also the largest party of the year: 165 million people partying for week. If you are here during carnival, be sure to get tickets for the Samba school tournament held at the *Sambodromo*, or wait till the Saturday after carnival and watch the top 5 schools parade (*Desfile das Campeãs*). See page 97 for more info.

MARCH

MOBILE COMPANIES MUSIC FESTIVALS

Different international brands have been sponsoring music events on Flamengo or Copacabana beach, hiring huge international bands to perform. Entrance is usually free.

SHIFTING IN MARCH

Holy week

BRAZIL-WIDE

Carnaporto- off season 6 day music fest/street party in Porto Seguro – BA

LEAVE RIO DURING NATIONAL HOLIDAYS

When planning your trip, watch out for national holidays, checking to see if they land close to a weekend. If so, be sure to make reservations to check out Buzios, Paraty, Ilha Grande or Petropolis, as Rio's elite flock to these places, making it much more fun than during off season.

EVENTS

APRIL

MAY

JUNE

PÁSCOA

Easter is a big event in Brazil, as this is a 90% catholic country. A national holiday occurs on Good Friday, so people tend to take the whole week off. Everyone goes somewhere, so if you are in Rio, it is a fun time to visit Buzios, Paraty or Ilha Grande.

21ST OF APRIL

Tiradentes Day (Independence hero)

23RD OF APRIL

Saint George Day (Only In Rio)

SKOL BEATS

A music festival sponsored by Skol, the beer brand. Lots of national and international artists.

1° DE MAIO- LABOR DAY

May 1st is Brazil's Labor Day, when no one works. Some larger parties and concerts may be sponsored by clubs or rave promoting companies.

PETRÔ-FANTASY

Just like Terefantasy: a costume party 1 hour outside Rio. Mostly frequented by Rio's college students. Beautiful venue, music and show.

Festa Junina

Festa Junina is a hick fest. Everyone dresses like a hillbilly and goes square dancing, Brazilian style of course. Usually these events are held between large groups of friends (100 or more), but some are run by a party promotion company. Worth a visit. Ask your concierge for the public ones sprinkled throughout the city.

CORPUS CHRISTI

Shifting in June.

BRAZIL-WIDE

Carnabelô

Belo Horizonte-MG

---

* TO GET MORE INFO ON THE ABOVE:

To find out when the next one is on, check for flyers outside clubs like Bunker, Six or Casa da Matriz. Also, check the "A2" adult store in Ipanema, as they tend to carry most of the flyers for the weekly parties and events.

You should also get the "Revista de Programa" on the Friday edition of the Jornal do Brasil newspaper and ask your concierge to find out what is going on as far as one-off events, shows and festivals.

YEARLY

JULY

WINTER FESTIVAL

Petropolis, Teresopolis and Friburgo host a 2 week winter festival (weekends mostly), with different shows, food stands, drinking etc.

SCHOOL VACATION

All month

BRAZIL-WIDE

Fortal - off season 4 day music fest/street party.

Fortaleza-Ce

www.fortal.com.br

AUGUST

BRAZIL-WIDE

Micarecandanga - off season 3 day music fest/street party.

Brasília-df

www.mondaymonday.com.br

JF-FOLIA

Off season 3 day music fest/street party in Juiz de Fora, in Minas Gerais

Www.jffolia.com.br

SEPTEMBER

RAVES

Raves come and go in Rio, as government pressure mounts to stop them. Look for their flyers at the locations listed on page 93, and check them out.

They are very different from 1st World raves: most are held in outdoor areas, country clubs or huge garden complexes.

7TH OF SEPTEMBER

Independence Day

TIM FEST

Sponsored by a phone company, this 4 day event takes place on the Museum of Modern Art, a beautiful venue, and given the steep price for the tickets, only Rio's affluent (or well connected) make it.www.angraeletrico.com.br

---

A WORD ON FREE EVENTS IN BRAZIL

If it is free, there will be at least a million people there. If it is good, another 2 million. If you are in Rio during the time a major free concert is taking place, ask for the paid venues and parties to watch it from: apartment, boat or schooner parties may cost you R$200 or more, but will guarantee you a safe time, less hassles and all you can eat and drink (usually). Don't skimp out.

EVENTS

OCTOBER

RAVES (CONT.)

The rave culture hasn't influenced people's fashion style yet, so you may see thousands of people wearing regular clothes. Also, the recreational drugs associated with raves (you know what I'm talking about) are scarce compared to London and Berlin. During the summer, look for beach raves along Ipanema after midnight.

12 OF OCTOBER

Our Lady of Aparition - Brazil's Holy Lady

BRAZIL-WIDE

Oktober Fest

The German beer drinking festival, run by Brazil's German community. What could be a better mix?

Blumenau, Santa Catarina

NOVEMBER

OI NOITES CARIOCAS

An unmissable series of big-name rock bands performing on top of Urca Hill, the one before Sugar Loaf, overlooking the city at night. The setting couldn't be better, the crowd very well selected and the ambiance is as cool and romantic as it gets. As soon as you get to Rio ask around for which bands are worth checking out as the styles vary. Shows going on between November and Carnival.

www.oinoitesCariocas.com.br

2ND OF NOVEMBER

Finados (Dead Day)

15TH OF NOVEMBER

Republic Proclamation Day

20TH OF NOVEMBER

Zumbi Dos Palmares : Black Consciousness Day

DECEMBER

NEW YEARS

NYE is huge in Rio. It is actually, the largest get together in the World: over 2 million people go to Copabacana beach to watch the fireworks shows. See page 93 for more info.

X-MAS

24th-25th Dec.

BRAZIL-WIDE

Carnatal - off season 4 day music fest/street party in Natal, RN.

www.carnatal.com.br

CARNIVAL

Carnival

The world's second largest party takes place in Rio, losing only to Salvador's carnival, which tops 2 million people on two avenues for 6 consecutive days. Rio gets packed with tourists from around Brazil and abroad, and the upper class residents leave to celebrate elsewhere, usually Buzios, Angra or Salvador.

WHAT IS CARNIVAL?

Carnival is an exuberant celebration of the carnal sins, as its Latin name suggests (carni=meat, val=galore). This developed due to the Catholic church's rule of demanding celibacy for 40 days before lent. What's the natural thing to do when you know you are going to starve? That's right, to stuff yourself! Carnival started in Florence, Italy and was soon picked up by the Portuguese living in Brazil centuries ago.

The Florentine feasts involved masks to keep party goers' identity and reputation intact. The feather costumes were influenced by the Brazilian

natives and the drums by the African slaves. Mix it all up, and never stop, and you get a 200 year tradition involving all the senses for the 5 days before Ash Wednesday.

THE SAMBA SCHOOLS

Despite the name, they are not schools but large membership clubs of musicians, costume designers, dancers and coordinators who spend 11 months of the year planning what show their school is going to put on during the next Samba championship.

They get a theme to work on in April, they start developing ideas for a parade in May, they start choosing the songs in August and start making the costumes in September. They rehearse till the end of January and present their parade in the *Sambodromo* during the weekend of Carnival, hoping to amaze the 4 judges in each of the 10 categories. The categories involve best lyrics, best drums, best costumes, best floats, best dancing, best melodies etc, similar to the Oscars.

On Ash Wednesday the voting is tallied and a winner is announced.

The top five schools then perform their parade again in the "champion's parade" on the following Saturday. Since the schools already won, this parade is looser and non-members can buy a costume to parade in it.

Parading in a samba school during carnival becomes one of life's most unforgettable experiences, so if you get a hold of a costume, by all means take it if you get a free one or buy it if you can afford it.

Prices for ground level costumes range from R$200 to R$700 depending on the school, whereas the float costumes can go for R$5000 (and you have to look super-model hot and know how to samba to be considered for possible inclusion). As far as getting an amazing experience for a decent price, the R$300 costumes will do. Once you get the costume, you'll be assigned an aisle from that samba school. The 4000

CARNIVAL

costumed members wait for an hour before going parading through the Sambodromo, a mile long stadium designed for this competition. The parading takes each school 80 minutes. Since you are instructed by the aisle leader to just "jump around and have fun", 80 minutes goes by quickly, as opposed to the memories.

THE SAMBODROMO

Should you not want to parade and to just watch the show, you have two options: the bleachers or the sky boxes:

THE BLEACHERS

This is where the masses go, despite the R$100 to R$300 price tag on the tickets. Being a first-timer, you won't have the Brazilian's patience to arrive early and wait all day saving the good seats. Beer is sold by beer-cooler yielding guys, so you don't have to move around the packed stadium too much. You can get tickets through your receptionist. If prices permit, opt for the 3, 5 or 7th sector, as these offer full views of the parade. The 1st sector is too close to the start to get a good view and the 9th is receded, offering only a partial view of the show.

THE SKY BOXES

The sky boxes are usually bought out by large corporations

to schmooze clients. Tickets can range from R$2000 to R$4000 for the 3 days of show. The views aren't anymore privileged than in the bleachers, just the food and drinks are more bountiful.

WHAT TO DO DAY AND NIGHT:

Street parties: Rio is sprinkled with little street carnival parties, where bands will play old-time favorites. Ask your concierge for the schedule and locations, as it is published until a few days before carnival.

Beach: Ipanema and Copacabana will be packed, and this is always the option before you start drinking.

Carnival Balls: An all out party with semi-orgy activities (no sex in public, but you know it's on when you bring him/her back). Ask your concierge for tickets. Some balls are filled with hookers, while most have regular people.

Samba School Parade at the Sambodromo: As mentioned above, get tickets and watch at least one night of the event.

FOR TICKETS AND COSTUMES

Rio Charm
Contact: Bryan
US 305 767 4525 or Rio 8606-7497
info@riocharm.com. Contact for prices or samba parade tickets, samba costumes, sky box tickets or NYE parties.

NEW YEAR'S EVE

New Year's Eve is a huge event anywhere, but it is special in Rio: its the worlds largest gathering. It usually records 2 to 3 million people on Copacabana beach (5 million during the millennium party). Traffic clogs up the city all night long, so don't plan on bar hopping that night. What to wear? All Brazilians celebrate NYE wearing white to ask Yemanja, the sea goddess, for peace. Don't come dressed in anything else as you'll look stupid, and if you didn't pack white clothes, buy some. Where should you party? All the clubs offer an "all inclusive special" from R$50 to R$300 pp. The more you pay, the more you get, the less you pay, the more you wait in line to get a beer. The club parties are fine, but if you make acquaintances with Brazilians, finagle your way into their party, preferably if it's in someone's flat facing Copacabana beach, so you can watch the fireworks show put on by the city. The cover price for most private "flat" parties also range from R$50 to R$300. What's also cool about the Copa flat parties is that you can party till 11:30pm, walk down to Copa beach to watch the fireworks with the masses, then come back to the party. Since most people woke up early and sat at the beach all day, most will be pooped by 4am, even with Redbull in their veins.

RIO NIGHTLIFE

CLUBS

The clubs found in this guide are usually frequented by Rio's elite, from 20 to 35 year olds. Clubs tend to be for the single crowd, where they go to not be single for that night. Cariocas like to arrive at clubs very late. Most clubs start around midnight, some even after 1am (Bunker, Casa da Matriz) This doesn't mean that they are at home waiting for the clock to strike twelve. Instead, they pre-party at the closest "botequim" for a warm-up.

There is no alcohol curfew, so bars and clubs close as soon as the house starts to empty. But since Cariocas are day creatures and have a beautiful day at the beach to look forward to, most places are empty by 5pm.

STREET PARTIES

These are places where different tribes congregate to hang out in the street, obviously with a beer in hand. You'll find a younger college crowd at most of these places. These are a great option if you want to talk to other Brazilians, and these events are easy on your wallet, as there is never any entrance charge and beers aren't marked-up.

LIVE MUSIC

We've listed the places with Brazilian music being performed by local musicians. No international pop or big concerts found here. Although these places offer a great cultural experience, they tend not to attract single people, especially during the week.

CHILLING

These are places where you can sit and enjoy a conversation with your friends, over drinks and bar finger-foods. Similarly, some of these are great for couples looking to get away from meat-markets and wanting a more casual evening.

BAR HOPPING AREAS

With the exception of Lapa and South side of Leblon, there are very few bar-hopping areas in Rio.

If, however, you want to paint the town red and visit several spots in one night, we recommend hiring a guide instead of cabbing back and forth.

LUAUS

There are hardly any luaus in Rio as Cariocas mysteriously tend to stay away from the beach at night (it could be a safety thing or the moisture ruining girl`s hair). Your chances are limited to January and February, when the weather is hot enough.

CONSUMPTION CARD SYSTEM

The control card most clubs hand you as you walk in is called a consumption card. The bartender marks on it what you

order. Before leaving the place, you go to the cashier and pay for everything you had. This way, you don't have to handle money during your night, nor do you tip in excess. They will add 10% as an automatic tip to the waiter. Note: Do not lose the card as they will fine you over R$100 to allow you to leave their establishment.

APPROACH INDEX:

The potential for approaching someone (or being approached by someone) is rated here on our personal experiences. 1= mostly couples, 5= mostly singles out on the hunt.

Sunday Night- Clubbing

BARONNETI

A designer interior and classy drinks sets this place apart. (ages 18 to 30) approach index: 3 Get there at: 11pm :: Dress up.
Rua Barão da Torre 354, Ipanema :: Also good on Fri & Sat

Sunday Night- Street Party

BAIXO GÁVEA

This is where every college student living in the Zona Sul (south side) is to be found on Sundays and Mondays. People hang out in the street from 6pm till midnight, on Mondays from 8pm to 1am. A guaranteed good time for all. (ages 18 to 30) approach index: 3 :: Dress casual. Baixo Gavea, Gavea :: Also good on Mon

Sunday Night- Live Music

CASA ROSA- SAMBA DA ALICE

Hidden in Laranjeiras neighborhood, Casa Rosa is the only fun place in this part of the city. It is a large house modified into a party house, with rooms, garden, pool tables, and lots of places for you to be naughty. On Sundays, they have the samba and pagode circles, where different bands will perform while more down-to-earth visitors will crowd around and sing along. A very different and relaxed atmosphere. (ages 20 to 30) approach index: 4 Get there at: 7pm :: Dress casual.

SPECIAL DEAL FOR OUR READERS CHECK BACK FLAP

Rua Alice 550, Laranjeiras :: Also good on Thu, Fri & Sat

Sunday Night- Chilling

COBAL LEBLON

A huge open-air patio filled with tables for Rio's bourgeoisie to go and gossip about their weekend exploits. Lots of beautiful people, unfortunately surrounded (and protected) by their beautiful friends. Great thin crust pizza. Well behaved. (ages 18 to 30) approach index: 1 Get there at: 10 pm :: Dress casual.

Cobal do Leblon, Leblon :: Also good on Fri & Sat

Rio For Partiers

Monday Night- Clubbing

NUTH

One of Rio's favorite clubs, with a very classy atmosphere, till it overpacks, then it bumps till the wee hours. We recommend you to get there early, before 10pm, as the line becomes monstrous very quickly. Or show up at 9pm and dine at their restaurant (the picanh burger is the best I've had). Monday night is for a mature crowd (40 to 60), but the rest of the week is for the young players. Dress up. (ages 20 to 35) approach index: 4 Get there at: 9pm

Av. Armando Lombardi 999, Barra :: Also good on Wed thru Sun.

Monday Night- Street Party

EMPÓRIO

Empório is one of those miracles marketing-gurus can't explain: without any promotion or marketing, they have been Ipanema's favorite street party place every day of the week, for the last 15 years. Monday is a good a night as any, lasting till 5am, always good for a last beer. (ages 18 to 30) Approach index: 4 Get there at: 11pm :: Dress down.

Maria Quitéria com Prudente, Ipanema :: Also good every day of the week

Monday Night- Live Music

SEVERYNA

A mixture of live music with dancing, Severyna is bumping the ultra corny Forro music, so corny it's fun. What's more, you dance so close together, Forro events have become a preferred spot for single people. (ages 31 to 50) approach index: 3 Get there at:10pm :: Dress casual.

Rua Ipiranga 54, Laranjeiras :: Live Music every day

Monday Night- Chilling

Must Experience

OVELHA NEGRA

SPECIAL DEAL FOR OUR READERS CHECK BACK FLAP

Brazil`s first "champagne only" bar. Friendly atmosphere and affordable bottles starting at R$25... you can`t go wrong. A great break from the beer and caipirinha scene. (ages 22 to 40) approach index: 3 Get there at: 7pm, closes at 11:30pm. :: Dress casual. Rua Bambina 120 Botafogo :: Also good on Tue to Fri

Tuesday Night- Clubbing

Zero Zero (00)

You can spend all night at 00 and not get bored. Rio`s creme de la creme hit this flawlessly designed modern lounge, part outdoor (mingling area) part indoor (tables), with cutting edge contemporary cuisine (try the salmon burger) and a tiny dance floor that fits everyone. Try a cigar on the asian chaises outside under the stars. (ages 25 to 35) approach index: 4 Get there at: 11pm :: Dress casual Av. Padre Leonel Franca 240, Gávea (Planetario) .:: Also good on Wed-Sat

Tuesday Night- Street Party

Beco do Rato

Real Brazilians having a real good time. Since it has no cover charge it becomes a street party. The samba musicians are often in Rio`s A-list. Dress down to fit in. Sing along and dance to Samba or try their "pastel de angu de carne", a beef turn-over made of corn mash. (ages 20 to 50) Approach index: 3 Get there at: 10pm Rua Joaquim Silva 11, Lapa .:: Also good on Wed-Sat

Tuesday Night- Live Music

HIDEAWAY

Jazz session starting at 10pm, allowing you to have a nice Brazilian style pizza before hand. Great ambiance. (ages 25 to 45) Approach index: 3 Get there at: 9pm

Rua da Laranjeiras 308, Laranjeiras:: Also good on Thu-Sat

SPECIAL DEAL
FOR OUR READERS
CHECK BACK FLAP

Tuesday Night- Chilling

THE IRISH PUB

What the hell is an Irish pub doing on a Brazilian tour route? Well, for one I live next door to it, so you may have a chance to kick my ass on any recommendations you disagree with. Gringos are great at making caipirinhas, so this is one place to test that theory. (ages 23 to 40) approach index: 2 Get there at: 9pm :: Dress casual.

Rua Jangadeiros 14a, Ipanema :: Also good on Fri & Sat

Wednesday Night- Clubbing

NIGHTLIFE

MARIUZINN

Mariuzinn has been around since the dinosaurs, and will be here till the alien invasion. Wednesday is Zouk dance night, which is a more sensual type of Lambada, the type where you get pregnant without knowing. It is always packed with a non-pretentious crowd. (ages 20 to 30). Approach index: 4 Get there at :10pm :: Dress casual.
Av N. S. Copacabana 435 , Copacabana :: Also good on Thu thru Sat

Wednesday Night- Street Party

PRAIA VERMELHA

The closest thing you'll get to a luau, since its on the beach right next to sugarloaf, in the safest area in Rio (Urca's military complex is around it). Free show of chorinho, pagode and samba by some of Rio's diehards. The latin simplicity: free music, panorama and cheap beer makes this one of the most important nightlife stops of your tour. Even if for an hour. (ages 20 to 70) Approach index 2 Get there at 9:30pm. Cancelled on rainy days. :: Dress casual. Praia Vermelha, Urca :: Also good on Mon and Fri

Wednesday Night- Live Music

RIO SCENARIUM

A live music saloon with three floors, a dance floor and a central balcony dispersing the music between them. It is beautifully decorated with antique items from 1910 to 1960, adding to its charmy ambiance. Lots of seating is available to those who arrive early. Apart from superb caipirinhas made from Magnifica cachaça, the joint also offers great finger food such as the "bijus". A must for anyone staying in Rio. (ages 25 to 60) approach index: 3 Get there at: 9pm :: Dress up.
Rua do Lavradio 20, Lapa :: Also good on Tue thru Sat

Wednesday Night- Chilling

PALAPHITA KITCH

Super zen Amazonian themed outdoor lounge facing sparkly Lagoa with lots of rustic sofas and benches, accommodating couples to groups. Amazonian finger foods and various flavored caipirinhas. (ages 26 to 40) approach index: 2 Get there at: 10pm :: Dress casual.
Kiosk da Lagoa (reta do Corte Cantagalo) :: Also good on Thu-Sat

Rio For Partiers

Thursday Night- Clubbing

GUAPO LOCO

The most famous Mexican food restaurant in Rio has its craziest nights for dancing on Tuesdays and Thursdays. On Saturdays and Sundays they have an all-you-can eat buffet for R$22. (ages 20 to 30) approach index: 5 Get there at: 8pm :: Dress Up.

Rua Rainha Guilhermina 48, Leblon
Rua Armando Lombardi 493, Barra ::
Also good on Tue, Fri & Sat

Thursday Night- Street Party

ARCO DO TELES

A series of after-work bars filled with downtown's "what-a-day-I-need-a-drink" crowd. (ages 21 to 50) approach index: 4 Get there at: 6pm :: Dress casual. Be sure to check out the live pagode at "Kamikase"...free!

Arco do Teles, Centro :: Also good on Wed & Fri

Thursday Night- Live Music

TRAPICHE GAMBOA

Although hard to find, it offers true samba, chorinho and pagode and a very bouncey dance floor. Up stairs lounge and outdoor patio up in the back ideal for hot nights. Worth checking out, specially since the finger food is well made. (ages 27 to 50) approach index: 2 Get there at: 10pm :: Dress casual.
Rua Sacadura Cabral 155 :: Also good on Fri-Sat

Thursday Night- Chilling

SATURNINO

Swanky martini bar in Jardim Botanico, filled with hip locals. Lots of variations on the caipirinha, so try them all. (ages 27 to 45) approach index: 3 Get there at: 9pm :: Dress nice.
Rua Saturnino de Brito 50, Jardim Botanico .: Also good on Wed-Sun

Friday Night- Clubbing

BARDOT

A New York style pocket-club that packs fast and boils fervently, with an intimate dance floor, food, bar and dining area. Rio`s finer dressed. (ages 27 to 40) approach index: 4 Get there at: 11pm :: Dress up. Rua Dias Ferreira 247 , Leblon :: Also good on Thu, Sat.

CASA DA MATRIZ

Imagine someone's house turned into a night club. 2 Dance floors, 2 bars, 1 shop, 1 movie room and a video game room! Yes, play all those games from your childhood drunk for free! Frequented by Rio's neo-hippie, students and the alternative crowd. Enjoy a few beers at the bar down the street while waiting for the place to warm up. (ages 18 to 30) Approach index: 4 Get there at: 1am :: Dress casual. Rua Henrique de Novais 107, Botafogo :: Also good on Wed thru Sun

Friday Night- Street Party

LAPA

Lapa is great any day of the week, specially on Fridays and Saturdays: you have a choice of over 12 bars and areas to hang out at, most of them with live Brazilian music. A most definite must (Ages 18 to 35) approach index: 4 Get there at: 10pm :: Dress casual.

RUA DO MERCADO

Happy hour central. A colonial part of downtown is the Rua do Mercado, which has pagode street parties every Friday evening. The area offers a dozen bars to hop around, with a square for the pagode get-together. (ages 20 to 40) approach index: 4 Get there at: 7pm Rua do Mercado, Centro

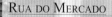

Friday Night- Live Music

BAR DA LADEIRA

One of the newest additions to the
Lapa area: a big house turned into a
live samba music joint. Great finger
food, cheap cover, lots of different
areas for you to get quaint in. (ages
28 to 50) approach index: 4 Get there
at: 9pm :: Dress casual. Rua Evaristo de
Veiga 149, Lapa :: Also good on Thu-Sat

BIP BIP

Another down and dirty dive where the locals come to jam various styles
of Carioca music, from samba to bossa nova to chorinho. Very authentic,
very mixed. (ages 20 to 50) approach index: 1 Get there at: 9pm :: Dress
casual. Rua Almirante Gonçalves 50, Copacabana :: Also good on Tue-Sat

Friday Night- Chilling

Devassa

Considered the best beer in Rio and possibly all of Brazil, Devassa is the answer to premium micro-brew. Apart from the lager, red, pale and stout, they have an exceptional food menu. There are Devassas popping up everywhere, so ask for the nearest one. (Ages 25 to 55) Approach index: 3 Get there at: 6pm :: Dress casual. Good everyday

Av. General San Martin 1241, Leblon
Rua Prudente de Morais 416, Ipanema
Av. Lineu de Paula Machado 696, Jardim Botânico

SPECIAL DEAL
FOR OUR READERS
CHECK BACK FLAP

SHENANIGANS

Whenever you feel home sick, just go to Shenanigans: it has Guinness and Newcastle, burgers, nachos, barbecue wings, baseball, football and soccer on the TV screens, pool (American table) and darts. Not only that, but the lion's share of its clients are gringos, so you can team up with them for your group excursions and sport activities. (ages 18 to 35) approach index: 4 Get there at: 9pm :: Dress casual.

Rua Visconde de Pirajá 112, Ipanema :: Also good everyday of the week

Saturday Night- Clubbing

CRISTAL LOUNGE

SPECIAL DEAL
FOR OUR READERS
CHECK BACK FLAP

One of Rio`s newest & ritziest clubs, located in Ipanema,
next to Baronetti and the Informal bar. Dress way up.
Rio`s prime DJs are here. Dance floor on first floor,
lounge on second, VIP tables on third. To get in fast, call
2247-8220 or 8267-4929 and ask for the Rio For Partiers
special, so you can save 20% on entrance. (ages 21 to 32)
approach index: 4 Get there at: 11pm :: Dress up.
Rua Barao da Torre 334, Ipanema :: Also good on Fri. Check site for the
rest of week. www.cristallounge.com.br

Saturday Night- Street Party

Must Experience

SALGUEIRO

Salgueiro samba school has won a lot of samba championships. At the same time, they are one of the clubs closest to the south side (R$24 cab from Ipanema to Salgueiro) and by far the safest. During their weekly rehearsals on Tuesdays and Saturdays, you won't see a fight, pick pockets or rude behavior, since the event is strictly sponsored by Rio's underground kingpin, who wants everyone to have a good time at his party. Hang out outside in the street party till midnight, then go in. Pricey entrance ($10 to $25), but worth it. (ages 20 to 40) approach index: 3 Get there at: 11pm :: Dress down.
Quadra do Salgueiro, Tijuca :: Only happening between August and Carnival

Rio For Partiers

Saturday Night- Live Music

CENTRO CULTURAL CARIOCA

Located right behind Lapa, CCC manages to get Rio's best bands to perform every day. You can go in blindly and have a great time. Great food and drinks. (ages 28 to 50) Approach index: 2 Get there at: 10pm :: Dress up. Rua do Teatro, 37 - Praça Tiradentes - Centro. :: Also good on Thu& Fri

FEIRA DE SÃO CRISTOVÃO

AKA Feira dos Paraiba, this arena has scores of bars, with live music stages on both ends, playing none other than cheesy *arrocha*, *forro* or *axé*. Extremely "latin" decorations makes this place anthropologically eye-opening. Ages 20 to 50. Approach index 4. Get there 9pm :: Dress casual. Feira de São Cristovão. :: Also good on Fri

Saturday Night- Chilling

BarCode

A bar build-in to a hostel, so there is always a young international crowd. Tons of new drinks and specials. Table area on the balcony or upstairs. Great place to meet other travellers. (ages 19 to 30) approach index: 4 Get there at: 9pm. Dress casual.
Rua Paul Redfern 48, Ipanema :: Also good on Thu & Fri

Ipanema Beach

One beautiful option right after the sunset is to bring a bottle of wine, a cork screw and 2 glasses (or plastic cups) and sit on the sand or any of the beach kiosks on Ipanema, or on Arpoador stone watching the beach. There are fishermen that never leave that area, so the place isn't deserted. Plus there are cops patrolling the beach front regularly. Bring cigars and what nots. Also look for luaus around posto 9 during the summer, as they tend to happen at least once a week. :: Dress down.

AFTER HOUR
FOODS & MOTELS

If you didn't hook up during your night out, you might as well go for a quick meal before crashing. There aren't a whole lot of sit-down breakfast or middle-of-the-night restaurants in Rio, so Cariocas turn to the hotdog stands or *caldo de feijao* (black bean soup) to absorb all those caipirinhas. The 4 most recommended spots are:

1 Pizzaria Guanabara, which has very cheesy and doughy slices of pizza, and has been a traditional after-hour hangout. If you didn't hook up and still got the energy, give this joint a try.

2 Cervantes: Every taxi-driver's favorite. The bartenders are the fastest at assembling a pineapple-steak-and-cheese sandwich: 7 seconds.

3 Hot-dog do Humaitá: you can spot the chef's hat from far away, and the hotdogs are pretty darn good.

4 Lamas: Easily the best US$3 steak sandwich (file mignon, mind you) you'll ever taste in the history of the world for ever and ever. True that.

Taxi-driver directions are in Portuguese.

Motel
"Bambina"
Rua Bambina

Motel
"Panda"
Rua São
Clemente pe
Dona Marta

Snacks
"Fornalha"
Rua Humaita
em frente ao
Ballroom

Hot Dog
"Cachorro quen
do Oliveira"
Rua Humaita em
frente Ballroom

Fast Food
"Bob's"
Rua Fonte da Saudade
com Lagoa, inside
"Shell" gas station

Fast Food
"Bob's"
Av. Borges de Medeiros
dentro do posto "Shell"

Fast Food
"BB Lanches"
Rua Ataulfo de Paiva
em frente Pizzaria
Guanabara

Pizza
"Pizzaria Guanabara"
Rua Ataulfo de Paiva
em frente BB Lanches

GAVEA

Motel
"Vip's"
Av. Niemeyer

Fast Food
"Mc Donald's"
Rua Ataulfo de
Paiva em frente
Praça Cazuza

LEBLON

Motel
"Toy"
Rua Maria
Luisa Pitanga

Motel
"Shalimar"
Av. Niemeyer
perto do Vidigal

Convenience Sto
"Padaria Rio Lisb
Av Ataulfo de Pa
com Venancio F

Motel
"Sinless"
Av. Niemeyer
perto do Vidigal

BARRA   SÃO CONRADO

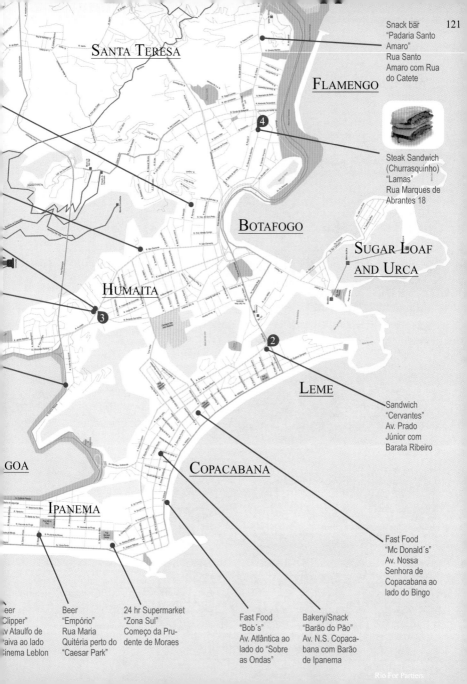

SANTA TERESA

FLAMENGO

Snack bār
"Padaria Santo
Amaro"
Rua Santo
Amaro com Rua
do Catete

Steak Sandwich
(Churrasquinho)
"Lamas"
Rua Marques de
Abrantes 18

BOTAFOGO

SUGAR LOAF
AND URCA

HUMAITA

LEME

Sandwich
"Cervantes"
Av. Prado
Júnior com
Barata Ribeiro

GOA

COPACABANA

IPANEMA

Fast Food
"Mc Donald's"
Av. Nossa
Senhora de
Copacabana ao
lado do Bingo

Beer
"Clipper"
Av Ataulfo de
Paiva ao lado
Cinema Leblon

Beer
"Empório"
Rua Maria
Quitéria perto do
"Caesar Park"

24 hr Supermarket
"Zona Sul"
Começo da Pru-
dente de Moraes

Fast Food
"Bob's"
Av. Atlântica ao
lado do "Sobre
as Ondas"

Bakery/Snack
"Barão do Pão"
Av. N.S. Copaca-
bana com Barão
de Ipanema

GAY

INTRODUCTION

Welcome to Rio, an exciting queer destination! It's a beautiful city with an exotic mix of sensual people who are gay-friendly and passionate. The city is teeming with excellent clubs, bars, parties and cultural events to suit any queer taste.

The focal point is the gay beach, just in front of Rua Farme de Amoedo, perhaps the gayest street of Rio, in the chic neighborhood of Ipanema; a place to relax and enjoy the view (and we're not referring only to sea and sand, mind you), and meet people. You'll soon see why the girl of Ipanema has been brushed aside by barbies (see queer types). Don't worry if you can't speak Portuguese, English and body-language is usually understood.

On weekends the beach in front of Copacabana Palace attracts a mature as well as a bear crowd.

There is more to Rio than bichas (gay men) on beaches, and if its parties you're after, then you're in for a treat. Every night you can club and party, the only problem is choice. There are circuit parties, like B.I.T.C.H, The White Party, X-demente, and events like Carnival, Pride, or New-Years Eve, which attracts many dancing queers.

There are the top attractions (besides barbies and lesbian-chic), like sugar loaf mountain and Christ, and if you're a culture vulture then Rio offers, lots of history, architecture, GLBT cultural events, like a film festival, theatre, and fascinating museums (and no, they don't have pin-up pictures, but interesting collection of art and artifacts).

Farme de Amoedo Beach

RIO

written by Dan Littauer
dan@gbrazil.com

Gay Day

Rio is a huge city with many neighborhoods to explore. To begin your stay, you'll visit the Christ statue, learn and explore the queer historical neighborhoods, and finally go on top (ahem!) of Sugar Loaf with the glamorous drag queen Lorna Washington and in between, a fantastic lunch in Porcão Rio where you can enjoy a panoramic view of Rio!

Another day can be leisurely spent in Ipanema, the gayest of all neighborhoods (even during the day)! It's particularly queer along the strip between the restaurant NewNatural, on Barao da Torre all the way to the beach in front of Farme de Amoedo street. In Ipanema you can find gay-friendly bars, clubs, cafes, theatres, cinemas, bookshops and shops.

RIO GAY HALF DAY

Tuesdays - min 4 people

Pick up at hotel around 10am.

Drive past several beaches until Prainha.

Another stop at Abricó nude beach.

Rio G-Tour Operator
3813-0003 or contato@riog.com.br
Price: R$85 pp

SPECIAL DEAL
FOR OUR READERS
CHECK BACK FLAP

RIO GAY FULL DAY

Friday - min 4 persons

Pick up at hotel around 9:30am

Drive past several beaches until Prainha.

Another stop at Abricó nude beach.

Lunch at Barreado Restaurant (drinks not included).

Return via Tijuca Forest stopping to absorb the view.
Rio G-Tour Operator
3813-0003 or contato@riog.com.br
Price: R$195 pp

Gay Night

Like to party? Rio won't disappoint you!

SUNDAY

Is beach day, all Cariocas enjoy walking at the seashore of Copacabana, Ipanema or Lagoa, after the beach head for Farme and spend time in Bofetada with the Barbies. The best club tonight is 00, where you can also enjoy a yummy dinner, and relax in a lounge. Another good option is Fosfobox, a great for the latest alternative house tunes, often with live bands.

MONDAY

Monday is a quiet evening in town, people are recovering from partying all through the weekend and then walking in auto-pilot to work in the morning. If you fancy a coffee then head for Cafeina and watch the boyz go by. For girls La Girl is open with a line up of DJs. Alternatively just go and boogie the night away in Spazio.

TUESDAY

Having a relatively chilled out Monday you are ready to party. One choice is to hang around Posto 6 bars and then move on to Le Boy's Xtravaganza, the best party in town on Tuesday. Here you can dance all night to

GAY

SATURDAY

This night hang around Baixo Leblon a gay friendly bohemian party of Leblon with lots of bars and restaurants that remain open until late. Explore the area around Cazuza Square. Then head off to Galeria which has an excellent party with DJ Dudu Candelot playing groovy house tunes. Dama de Ferro has an excellent night with invited DJs, sometimes from abroad, often with very alternative house and techno tunes.

RIO GAY NIGHT

Thursdays - min 3 people

Pick up at hotel around 8pm

Guided tour around Lapa

Stop at "The Copa" bar for dinner and clubbing till 1am.

Rio G Tour Operator
3813-0003
contato@riog.com.br

Price: R$195 pp

CLUBS & BARS:

Bunker
R.: Raul Pompéia, 94 - Copacabana
tel: 2521-0367

Clube Radar
Rua Marechal Mascarenhas de Moraes, 191 – Copacabana

Bombar Redux
Rua General San Martin, 1011 - Leblon

the latest tunes, and watch a drag show and sometimes also go-go boys.

WEDNESDAY

You can wine and dine in The Copa, with ambient music, and then go dancing in various venues. If you like 80's music then head for Spazio, alternatively a few blocks away is Le-Boy with a Drag Show (usually Suzy Brazil), go-go boyz and stripper contest. If you want just a relaxing drink then head for Bar d'hotel in Leblon where you can also enjoy an excellent dinner.

THURSDAY

Is a great day to hang out especially in Ipanema. At around midnight, leave Farme De Amoedo Street and walk one block away to Teixeira de Melo, for Galeria. You can always have a drink in the bar outside, or just go straight to the excellent party in Galeria with a DJ LC that plays ambient 70's to 80's music. Alternatively go to Dama de Ferro for excellent house and alternative tunes, and watch for special events.

FRIDAY

Friday is the day for Lapa, a very queer friendly antique neighborhood with fabulous atmosphere! Have something to eat in Nova Capela, and then just hang around the pedestrian street Joaquim Silva; it turns into a huge street party, gay and straight, young and old, sambistas and DJs, hip-hop and funk musicians, make for some of the fascinating crowds that you will join.

RIO

Casarão Cultural Dos Arcos
Rua Mem Sá, 23 - Lapa

Galeria Café
Rua Teixeira de Melo nº 31 Ipanema

La Cueva
Rua Miguel Lemos, 51 Copacabana

Le Boy
Rua Raul Pompéia102 Copacabana

La Girl
Rual Raul Pompéia 102 Copacabana

Dama de Ferro
Rua Vinicius de Moraes 288 Ipanema

A Casa da Lua
Rua Barão da Torre 240-A Ipanema

The Copa
Rua Aires Saldanha 13-A Copacabana

Blue Angel
Rua Cinco de Julho 15-B Copacabana

Fosfobox
Rua Siqueira Campos 140 / 22-A
Copacabana

00 ZeroZero
Rua Pe Leonel Franca 240 Planetario
/ Gavea

Turma OK
Rua do Resende 43 Lapa

Cabaret Casa Nova
Av. Men de Sá 25 Lapa

Buraco de Lacraia
Rua André Cavalcante 58 Lapa

Cine Ideal
Rua da Carioca 65 Centro

For more info visit:
www.gbrazil.com
www.riog.com.br

RESTAURANTS & CAFÉS:
see dinner options on page 138

SAUNAS:
Studio 64
Rua Redentor 64 Ipanema

Sauna Copacabana
Rua Dias de Rocha 83 Copacabana

Thermas Leblon
Rua Barão da Torre 422 Ipanema

Le Boy
Rua Raul Pompéia 102 Copacabana

Projeto SB
Rua 19 de Fevereiro 162 Botafogo

Thermas Catete
Rua Correia Dutra 34 Catete

Kabalk – Sauna
Rua Santa Luzia 459 Maracanã

Rio G Spa
Rua Teixeira de Melo 16, Ipanema

Glossary

Want to fit into the scene? Let us give you some Gayducation about life in Rio!

Bicha: a colloquial word used by GLBT for gay man.

Barbie: probably the most famous *bicha*, one that loves to exhibit his muscular body so-called aptly after the famous doll.

Suzy: is an older doll that preceded *Barbie*, and hence denotes an ageing Barbie. Much like a *Barbie* until you hit the wrinkles (if they haven't been plastically remodeled), and the salt and peper muco - hair line (if there remains any).

Bicha Pintosa, also known as *qua-quá* an effeminate *bicha*, typically attempts to dress in trendy clothes, and often uses bikini on the beach in a manner that would make most girls look modest.

Bicha Fina: a *bicha* who wants to appear super sophisticated. This kind of a man thinks at the very least that he is Queen Victoria, all the rest please bow or move aside… and no, you are not watching AbFab!

Bicha Cult: a *bicha* pretending to be an intellectual, typically with his nose held high. He can quote you Sartre or Lacan but actually never read them, constantly talks about French movies and the latest thing from Europe.

GAY

Poc-poc: a *bicha* pretending to be trendy, but doesn't have the $$. He leaves the suburban bus hastily and then calmly walks to the club complaining about the taxi ride from the posh neighborhood of São Conrado

Tia (literally, auntie) also known as *bicha velha* is a term applied to older gays, particularly the ones who are slightly effeminate and refined.

Free-willy: a fat bicha. A rare specimen on Ipanema beaches as he is in danger of being confused with a whale, wouldn't want to scare them barbies would you? Just imagine all the commotion…

Sapa or Sapatão: (literally, a big shoe) a colloquial word used by GLBT for lesbian.

Caminhoneira: The traditional butch

Fanchona: This *sapa*, has typically short hair, short nails, uses tight trousers (mostly jeans) and likes to be direct and argue.

Lesbian Chic: a girly and sophisticated lesbian that actually does use lipstick! A champagne glass is permanently attached to their hand.

Other types to look out for:

Trava: a transsexual or transvestite. She has the most amazing boobs that make Cicciolina look like Shirley Temple when she was five years old.

Brazil
SAO PAULO PRIDE

Sampa for short is the right place to be when talking about Gay Pride!!

More than three million queers participate in this city's Pride, making it the biggest and most spectacular in the world! Meet many queer folk at the downtown Fair, or go to shopping in Oscar Freire street, the most fashionable shopping area of Latin America. Checkout the largest gay and lesbian scene in Latin America with GBrazil. But don't strain

yourself too much because you'll need your legs to boogie during the night in more nightclubs and parties, just let GBrazil guide you, bears, circuit, girlies, muscle-boyz, let us know and we'll get you there! Ready to let your hair down? Wanna show off your hours of labour at the gym? Then come to play around the Gay Day in the nearby amusement park. Then after that its time to party once more!

And last but not least (plenty of time for your beauty sleep), enjoy SãoPaulo Pride!!! Drag-queens, boyz, girlz, bears, leathermen, queer and straight families dancing and having fun in this huge march, including

RIO

floats; you've got the be there to be queer. G Brazil can provide you an all inclusive package, including flights, hotels, transfers and queue jumping tickets to a party starts for as little as US$250 per person.

FLORIANÓPOLIS

This gorgeous gay friendly beach city in the South of Brazil deserves a visit during summer season. Florianópolis, affectionately known as Floripa, is the gay friendly State capital of Santa Catarina. Famous for its beautiful bridge, that reminds one of San Francisco, this is a delightful and pretty city divided by the bay, half of it located the magical

Santa Catarina Island while the other is mainland. Explore the beautiful gay ocean beaches of Praia Mole and Galheta. Take a boat along the North Bay so that you can visit and enjoy the beautiful beaches and cute little islands just off this pleasant and friendly city. Besides, in summer there are many parties to explore! New Year's Eve is a must, and Carnaval here is so gay that a queer dressed

in pink would look rather dull. But wait, during the Brazilian spring time Floripa boats a fantastic gay pride along with the diversity games event – a sporting event for all the queer dudes and dudettes. An all inclusive GBrazil package, including flights, hotels, transfers and queue jumping tickets to a party starts for as little as US$300 per person.

SALVADOR DA BAHIA

Experience the magic of the goddess Yemanjá, at Salvador da Bahia. There you will hear all about its history of this amazing city founded in 1549, once the Brazilian colonial capital for more than two centuries. Then walk around the well preserved historical centre named "Pelourinho", and enjoy its extraordinary baroque architecture.

Discover how the Africans were able to keep the cults of their tribal religions using elements of the Catholic religion. Also don't miss the Bahian women (Baiana) dressed in white clothes, always with a wide smile together with their trays of candies and "acarajé"; a typical scene in almost every square in the lively city of Salvador. Salvador will offer you delightful and unique gastronomy of Bahia, based on African recipes with American ingredients, as well as a sizzling

gay and lesbian scene.

Visit one of the dozens of charming city beaches or short excursions to the many islands and beaches dotted in the beautiful bay of Todos os Santos. Then there are also gay beaches and charming colonial cities, as well as the beautiful island of Morro de Sao Paulo, all nearby for you to enjoy and explore. For all this and more let GBrazil provide you an all inclusive gay travel solution of: flights, gay friendly hotels and tours, clubs and events, transfers and guides, starting for as little as US $250 per person.

These are just some of the gaystinations you can visit with GBrazil with specifically designed packages for the queer traveler, including flights, gay friendly hotels, tours, clubs and much more!

TRAVEL SERVICES

To travel within Brazil to other gay destinations, for gay friendly hotel bookings or to find out about special gay tours or events within Rio, contact Dan at GBrazil and ask for the scoop.
GBrazil
Contact: Dan Littauer
dan@gbrazil.com
www.gbrazil.com
Rua Farme de Amoedo 76/303 Ipanema
2247-4431

HOW TO DEAL WITH

By India Lee Borba

We have all heard of `Latin Lovers,` but what does that mean exactly? Here are some of the answers to questions you may have about Brazilian men.

Brazilian women usually meet men through mutual friends. So, get out there and make some Brazilian friends. You never know who they could introduce you to. Brazilians are open, friendly and helpful people, and when it comes to conversation, Cariocas have no shame. So, exchange phone numbers or emails and make plans to meet up again.

In Brazil, the men are very fond of public affection and are romance experts. So, grab a caipirinha and ask someone to teach you to dance the Samba or Forró. Get ready to be close, because the Brazilians will have it no other way when it comes to dancing.

The men will tell you how beautiful you are, or for that matter, that you are the most beautiful woman they have ever seen!

Don't be surprised if you are lip-locked within the first 5 minutes of your conversation and be advised about the motels. Remember, that in Brazil, motels are for one thing, and one thing only. Sex! You have the power to accept the proposal or not, but just know what you are agreeing to.

No matter which type you choose, the important thing is to have fun and don't go falling in love on the first night!

When you are trying to relax on the beach, you are sure to be approached by at least one of the types, most likely, the Hippie. These docile men, will try to sell you a necklace or maybe even make you a free ring that costs less than 50 cents. But, it's the thought that counts, right?

If you are in a bar or club, a man may even send over his friend to tell you he thinks you are cute or send a note! This may sound juvenile to you, but it is considered normal here in Brazil.

Don't feel obligated to speak to every man who comes your way. If the men think that you are easy, you will be batting them away the whole evening which can get quite annoying.

DOS AND DON'TS

Here are a few dos and don'ts that should help you along.

• Don't hesitate to accept the offer of a kiss from any man who strikes your fancy.

• Do come armed with a pen and paper to ensure you will be able to pass out your phone number and email address, but don't expect them to call the next day.

• Do keep a positive attitude and play it cool when the annoying guy at the end of the bar won't take a hint and give up.

• Do ask a cute Carioca to show you around their beautiful city.

• Don't believe them when they tell you that you are the women of their dreams no matter how much you want to.

• Don't be surprised if you go to the motel and your man pays for it by the hour.

BRAZILIAN BOYS

Brazil is full of these beautiful, tan, athletic ´eye candy` and they come in 4 different flavors. In Rio there is the Preppy-type (wannabe playboy), the Pitboy , the Neo-hippie and the Player.

Reminder: These are generalizations and should not be taken too seriously.

THE PREPPY

Surfer by day, surfer by night. The Preppy-types always wear club clothes and a pretty face. They might even spend more time in front of the mirror getting ready to go out than you! At night, this type can usually be found in the hottest clubs of the moment, and during the day on the beach in Zona Sul (South Zone) playing football (soccer) or foot-volley. The Preppy is the most common type around.

THE PITBOY

The Pitboy is the type you will see almost as often as the Preppy, especially around Zona Sul. These Vin Diesel types are dedicated to their bodies. They are strong and tan and usually choose Jiujitsu as their favorite sport. You can probably guess what comes next. When you mix a lot of testosterone, alcohol and lack of women with a jiujitsu master...

Yes, a few Pitboys, true to nature, are unstoppable in fights. Watch out!

THE NEO-HIPPIE

If you prefer love and not war, I would recommend going with the Neo-hippie.

Although, these artsy-fartsy types are the least common, there are still plenty to choose from in Lapa and Santa Teresa. This type usually lives wherever the wind blows them, and they prefer peacefully sitting on the beach making jewelry, singing and socializing as their favorite sports.

THE PLAYER

Last, but not least, we have the Player who can also be found on the beach in Zona Sul jumping in for an occasional game of foot-volley, but usually prefers talking about money and how to make more of it! These are the eligible bachelors and ultimate players. They know what we want, and they have the ability to give it to us.

HOW TO DEAL WITH

All Carioca girls whole-heartedly believe they are the Girl From Ipanema. This means their ego is inflated. Some of the time they have every right: they look drop-dead gorgeous, work out, have incredible butts, nice hair and tans.

To make things worse, Carioca boys are always reminding them of how hot they look. These boys are very aggressive in their approach to seduction, meaning these women have had to build a hard shell around them, otherwise they would be picked up left and right and end up being treated like an object.

The worst places to meet them are on the street, where they are scared to death of being harassed or robbed, and at the beach, where they are surrounded by people they know (since they have frequented the exact same spot their entire lives) and don't want to ruin their reputation by seeming "easy" to strangers.

A great place for foreigners to meet friendly single women are the happy hour bars downtown, like Dito&Feito (Rua do Mercado), Pampa Grill, Arco do Teles and the bars in Lapa.

Most of these women still live with their parents, since Rio is a dangerous city for a girl to live alone. This means that you won't be invited back to their place. You will, however, get to kiss them within 30 minutes of talking with them, sometimes a lot faster than that. If things go really well and the chemistry works out, you can take them to a motel for a two hour session. (See our motel list on page 120). But just a reminder: kissing them does not guarantee that you will be sleeping with them, as it is common in Europe and the US. You may be making out with a serial kisser.

Should you catch yourself in a more meaningful conversation with a Brazilian girl, your next move is naturally to shag. Since there are no love nooks in Rio, like cute little alleys, safe parks or beaches, your best bet is to bring her back to your hotel (if the reception hasn't mentioned any policies against that) or to take her to a motel. Since you are probably moving around in a cab, the procedure is to tell the cab driver which motel you want to go to while she is stepping in the car. That way she won't feel embarrassed. A good one to memorize is "Motel VIP's" (pronounced "vee-pees"), close to Leblon.

Meanwhile, should she not want to sleep with you, she may ask for her digits or email. Unfortunately, it is probably unlikely anything will develop, since most of these girls have no problem finding a boy for their night the next time they go out.

What does all this mean for you? This means your approach should take some of these factors into consideration:

1) Don't hit on them at the beach, unless the beach is relatively empty. (Forget it on weekends.)

2) Don't bother trying to pick them up in the street.

3) Do come with a different approach to Carioca boys': try softer yet persistent. Instead of breaking their "pick-up resistance shell", try to melt it with a smooth approach. They may blow you off or ignore you at first, but keep at it and don't give up. Soon they will show their true selves.

4) A good conversation starter is to ask them about their opinion on touristy spots. Show this book and ask them what they recommend.

5) Do try to make out as soon as you can.

6) Don't insist on going back to their place. Do suggest a drive along Avenida Niemeyer (where most of the better motels are).

BRAZILIAN WOMEN

The Main Types

The 4 types of Brazilian woman (other than the normal family girl):

THE DADDY'S GIRL:

They are daddy's little girl, they dress like Christina Aguilera, they look great but they don't let anyone hit on them. Why? They have a huge waiting list of suitors from their former high-school, their college, their parent's friend's sons etc etc. They CAN be stuck up. Forget them, unless you are introduced to one.

THE POPOZUDA:

Round-butted sex bombs that look like the She Hulk. They work out, wear tight work out pants and do their best to look like a bomb-shell. Good to invest your time on... if you look good and buff too. Other wise forget it.

THE HIPPIE/RAVER:

The fun chicks, easy to approach, easy to talk to, hard to kiss, fun to party with.

THE 30 YEAR OLD

Wants to have fun, to dance, and to drink. Treat them like a lady and they will treat you like a king. Great option to hang out with.

SAFETY TIPS

As a general rule, gringos are somewhat untouchable on drug-lord rules. Your chances of being kidnapped, held hostage, etc are a lot smaller than that of an upper class Brazilian. But regardless, drug lords' powers are confined to only the smarter or bigger crooks. The small fish, such as young pick-pockets and out-of-town criminals, take their chances.

Beware on empty streets just as much as at overly crowded events. The new age in pick pocketing (some new Eastern-European techniques are now arriving in Brazil) is to create a situation in a crowd where your hands are distracted while they go for your pockets.

A good example is the Russian mustard trick, where they put mustard on your head in the subways. While you check to see what the heck is on your head, they go through your pockets.

Another common trick here in Brazil is the "fight breaks out" trick, when right in front of you there is a scuffle in the middle of a crowd. While everyone is being pushed away from the scuffle, and while you are holding someone who is being pushed onto you, someone behind you (sometimes a woman) goes through your pockets.

Don't be a hero: if you are held at gun point, slowly pass over the money and leave it at that.

Get the hell out after any dangerous situation: if you managed to stop a pick pocket in his tracks, get out, as his partners may come after you.

Another very common technique is for the crook to rob while on a bike. They can snatch your cellular phone, necklace or purse while passing by at high speeds.

If you are passing by a shady character in an empty street at night, wave an eager "Hi! I'm over here!" to your imaginary friend that's a block away. This should throw a monkey wrench in his scheme at the last second.

Don't trust the cops' intelligence or integrity: if you get pick-pocketed, say what-the-hell and go on with your tour instead of getting caught up in reporting incidents and other red tape. Not only is that an exercise in futility, but it will eat up your time and mood. Like a friend of mine said after getting $200 pick-pocketed in the north of Brazil: "Fuck it, I consider it a small tourist tax" and went back to drinking. Not the best point of view as a long-term philosophy, but it worked fine that week.

How to avoid being a target

As a general rule, you want to dress down. The grungy look will do you good. Since you are on vacation, you don't need to worry about your reputation or poor service. Here are some general rules to abide by, to better guarantee your safety (especially when anywhere between Flamengo and Centro or the north side):

BASEBALL CAPS
Dead give-aways.

HAIR CUT
Leave the "out of control" waxed hair style for the trendier clubs.

ACCENT
When in a crowd of dubious types, keep your talking to a minimum.

SHIRT
T-shirt instead of a Hawaiian shirt. Leave the Brazilian soccer team shirt for back home.

MONEY & IDS
Don't bring too much nor too little money, as they will shake you down till they get something. Don't carry a passport, nor all your credit cards or more than R$200. Bring one major CC and one form of ID: student, drivers' license or state. Don't trust your pockets, keep them zipped or buttoned up.

CAMERA
Don't walk around thinking the strap will guarantee your camera's safety.

BERMUDAS SHORTS AND FLOOD PANTS
You can wear bermudas shorts, but wear the styles the Brazilian boys wear, not what's in style back home. Flood pants never caught on in Rio, so no.

SANDALS
Wear tennis shoes or flip-flops instead.

Gringo

BRAZILIAN FOOD

B razilian traditional cuisine uses a wide variety of readily-available ingredients. But most are cooked with simple culinary techniques: boil it or fry it. This makes the different dishes seem almost rudimentary and very 18th Century. At the same time, most of the ingredients are rich in flavor, and therefore do not need complicated culinary improvement.

The three most traditional dishes, "Feijoada", "Bacalhoada" and "Tutu à Mineira" were all "slave" foods: rich in carbohydrates, proteins and fat, all needed to compensate for excessive manual labor. Due to their rich flavor, they were eventually adopted by all social classes.

Bahian food has a flavourful African influence, consisting mostly of sea food, beans, coconut milk and palm oil.

The *Churrasco* is of Argentinean influence. With the exception of salt, the meats are cooked with no spices or sauces, because the chef wants to show his guests that the quality and flavor of the meat does not need to be camouflaged.

At the same time, sugar cane cultivation had a strong effect on desserts: traditional Brazilian desserts are nothing more than fruits blended with tons of sugar. Most of these can be eaten along with cheese.

The contemporary-cuisine chefs in Brazil are making an impressive rediscovery of local ingredients, by adding new twists to old recipes, or inventing new dishes altogether and finally discarding the French school.

COMIDA A KILO

Food by the pound. You pile your plate from the buffet, weight it, and pay on weight. Prices range from $10 to $38 per kilo.

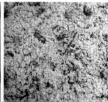

Popular Lunch Dishes

ALMOCO EXECUTIVO

(Executive Lunch): A cheaper version of the entrées offered at that restaurant, normally served during lunch. No suit and tie needed.

GALETO

Grilled game hen, a smaller, juicier cousin of the chicken. Usually served with pan fries (*batata portuguesa*), garlic bread and vinaigrette.

SANDUICHE DE FILET

Filet mignon on bread.

PF (PRATO FEITO)

Daily dish. Beans, rice, meat (chicken, steak, fish or pork), salad and fries or potatoes: the typical lunch dish eaten by 150 million Brazilians. Coincidentally, it is an incredibly well balanced diet of carbs, protein, fat and fiber.

PRATO DE VERÃO

Tropical Fruit Dish made of various fruits, ham, cheese and maybe a boiled egg.

BAURU

Open steak sandwich with fries, ham, fried egg and salad

Recommended Lunch Places

BRASILEIRINHO

True authentic brazilian country cooking, with all the trimmings Brazilians love. They now serve the following for around R$15: bean soup for starters, main course: ground beef, shoestring potatoes, fried egg, rice, beans, salad or mayoed legumes, farofa. Dessert: banana or guava sweet with minas cheese.

Rua Jangadeiros 10, Ipanema tel: 2513-5184

SPECIAL DEAL
FOR OUR READERS
CHECK BACK FLAP

DELÍRIO TROPICAL

A great salad restaurant for health nuts and normal people alike: you choose two or three sides of greens (caesar, green leaves, nicoise,etc), then you choose the main protein (salmon, salisbury steak, chicken, fish etc). Unmissable.

Rua Garcia D'avila 48, Ipanema
Rua da Assembléia 36A, Centro
Av das Américas 4666 - food court, Barra Shopping

GAROTA DE IPANEMA/COPA/URCA

A favorite and therefore a must: Picanha Brasileira. Don't bother looking at the menu. A pound of sliced raw top sirloin for you to fry to your liking, over a blazing hot iron skillet. Feeling confident? Ask for a side of raw garlic ("ali-o crew"), to fry over the skillet. Warning: highly addictive.

Rua Vinicius de Moraes w/ Prudente, Ipanema
Av Atlantica 3744, Copacabana
Av. Jõao Luis Alves 56, Urca

GALITOS GRILL

Another top-notch lunch place: For R$8 you get half a chicken with three sides. Ask for their top secret buttered-hot sauce ("manteiga de pimenta").

Rua Farme de Amoedo w/ Visconde de Piraja, Ipanema

TRADITIONAL

CHURRASCO

Churrasco is a popular Brazilian style barbecue that offers a wide variety of different cuts of beef, pork, lamb, chicken and fish, which are slowly cooked on special grills to preserve all their natural juices and flavors. *Churrascarias* are restaurants that serve endless rounds of meats on an all-you-can-eat basis, with drinks and desserts served separately. The most sought after meat is the "picanha", aka top sirloin, Brazil's favorite cut due to its blend of softness and flavour. Ideal for those nights you want to treat yourself to lots of good food. Porção, Rio's most famous all-you-can-eat steakhouse chain, also offers sushi and fish, as well as scores of side dishes and salads. Everyone's extremely pleased.

WHERE TO EAT: PORÇÃO   SPECIAL DEAL FOR OUR READERS CHECK BACK FLAP

Rua Barao da Torre 218, Ipanema
Porção Rios :: Aterro do Flamengo
Av. Armando Lombardi 591, Barra
For reservations call 3389-8989

FEIJOADA

Probably the most typical dish from Brazil: a black bean stew with hearty sausages and sundried beef, served with rice, collard greens, cassava (manioc) flour and orange slices. This may slow you down on the dance floor. Casa da Feijoada's specialty. A "must" experience. Feijoada with *caipirinha* go together like Starsky & Hutch, sticks & clutch. Ask for one from the oak-barrel aged "Vendaval" brand *cachaça*.

WHERE TO EAT: CASA DA FEIJOADA

Rua Prudente de Morais 10, Ipanema
tel: 2247-2776 :: 11 am to 1am   SPECIAL DEAL FOR OUR READERS CHECK BACK FLAP
www.cozinhatipica.com.br

Brazilian Cuisine

Seafood

There are two dishes in this restaurant that make it worth coming back: the first is the "pargo" fish in a rock salt mount, served with rice or potatoes. The rock salt is not used to season but to cook the fish at an even temperature, allowing the meat to end up equally white, suave, moist and flaky, as opposed to dark and dry on the sides and under-cooked in the middle. "Pargo no sal grosso" is the name. The second is the Bahian Shrimp Muqueca, a shrimp-coconut milk stew to die for. Worth checking out during the day and night, as it's outdoor tables view Ipanema and Leblon beaches.

Where to Eat: Azul Marinho

Av. Francisco Behring, Arpoador (Ipanema) tel: 2513-5014
All week 12pm to 12am
www.cozinhatipica.com.br

SPECIAL DEAL
FOR OUR READERS
CHECK BACK FLAP

Buffet

Those wishing to savor a little of the various Brazilian flavours can do so in one special place. Consecutively winning the "Buffet by the pound" category by most papers and critics, the Laskowsky family and its 72+ employees set the pace in Rio for food and service quality with great prices. You can choose to "help yourself" and pay by the pound or opt for the all-you-can-eat buffet. In either option you can treat yourself to oysters, shrimps, salmon, seafood, filet mignon, sushi, fresh green salads, and over 20 delicious home made desserts.

Where to Eat: Fellini

Rua General Urquiza 104, Leblon
All week 11am - 12am
tel: 2511 3600
www.fellini.com.br

SPECIAL DEAL
FOR OUR READERS
CHECK BACK FLAP

Major credit cards accepted unless stated.

FOOD

TRENDY BRAZILIAN

DESIGNER

We call it designer because apart from being super tasty the plates
look like works of modern art. The award-winning Ludmilla, the
head-chef at Zuka, has some of the most creative presentations for
her international mix restaurant, serving everything
from Brazilian classics to Thai satays to French
nouveau. Bring a camera as you will want to
photograph, print in large format and frame these true
works of art.

WHERE TO EAT: ZUKA

Be sure to make reservations as it quickly packs on weekends.
Rua Dias Ferreira, 233 Leblon :: tel: 3205-7154
Mon 7pm-1am, Tue- Fri 12pm-4pm & 7pm-1am; Sat 1pm-1am,
Sun 1pm-midnight

SPECIAL DEAL
FOR OUR READERS
CHECK BACK FLAP

PIZZA

Every place has a different definition of the ideal pizza: Chicago likes deep dish,
California likes medium thick, Italians like it thin. Brazilians like it extra thin
and large, baked in pine wood burning oven, for a crackly edge. Little tomato
sauce, extra cheese. See if they have it right. Hideaway is famous for its
pizza, as well as its dance floor packed with the young and
hip Zona Sul crowd.

WHERE TO EAT: HIDEAWAY

Rua Das Laranjeiras 308, Laranjeiras :: tel: 2285-0921
Tue -Thu + Sun 6pm to 2am, Fri+Sat 6pm 5am

SPECIAL DEAL
FOR OUR READERS
CHECK BACK FLAP

Major credit cards accepted unless stated.

CUISINE

ROMANTIC

Zazá Bistro, a cute little corner house decorated to South Asian chic is an ideal
for couples as well as for groups of friends. The downstairs has a little balcony
and interior with tables, while the upstairs is pillows and rugs surrounding
Moroccan tables where you can take off your shoes. The
menu is light and balanced, pursuing combinations
between flavorful spices such as ginger, lemon grass
and curry with healthy, non-fried organic foods.
The ambient music deserves a mention, as well
as the traditional and exotic drinks from the
experienced bartenders.

WHERE TO EAT: ZAZÁ BISTRO
Rua Joana Angelica 40, Ipanema :: tel:2247-9101
Sun-Thu 7:30pm - 12:30am, Fri-Sat 7:30pm-1:30am

SPECIAL DEAL
FOR OUR READERS
CHECK BACK FLAP

CONTEMPORARY

Zero Zero is the author's favorite restaurant+club in Rio: you can
have a delicious dinner inside or outside, then sit in the outdoor
terrace under the stars, digest with a cigar, then head over to their
tiny dance floor (the best type) and party when the DJ warms
up. Everything on their menu is finessed. There newly
opened sushi-bar is very popular amongst Rio's
mature clubbers.

WHERE TO EAT: 00 (ZERO ZERO)
Rua Padre Leonel Franca 240, Gavea (Planetario)
tel: 2540-8041
All week 8pm - 1am

WORLD

PORTUGUESE

Portuguese seafood is so common-place during family celebrations that it could be considered Brazilian gastronomical culture. The most famous and requested portuguese dish is the Bacalhau, cod fish, accompanied by potatoes, peppers, olives and onions. CBF made the cut in the book for a few reasons: 1) It is owned by one of the main importers of cod fish, so you know you`ll be getting prime product; 2) It has picnic bench tables, which are rare yet ideal for groups of friends; 3) it serves paella and other spanish dishes too; 4) it is 2 minutes from Rio Scenarium, so you can hop over saving on cab.

WHERE TO EAT: CBF
Praça Tiradentes 83, Centro :: tel: 2232-3215
Mon-Sat 11am till midnight or last client

SPECIAL DEAL
FOR OUR READERS
CHECK BACK FLAP

MEXICAN

WTF? Mexican? Yup, good old burritos, tacos, quesadillas, fajitas, enchiladas and nachos. Margaritas! What`s best is that after you eat, you can stay and party, as the restaurant becomes a club later on in the night. All available at Guapo Loco, Rio`s finest and funnest mexican joint.

WHERE TO EAT: GUAPO LOCO
Rua Rainha Guilhermina 48, Leblon :: tel: 2495-2995
Av Armando Lomabardi 493, Barra :: tel: 2495-2995
Mon-Sun 19pm till last client
Rio Sul Mall, food court on 2nd floor :: tel: 2541-3726
Restaurant only, no club. Noon till 9pm

SPECIAL DEAL
FOR OUR READERS
CHECK BACK FLAP

FOODS

JAPANESE

Japanese food is huge in Rio. Women love it since it is very light while tasty. Guys love it because the women are there. Benkei is cool because "It's all you can eat"! That's right, for under R$40 you can eat all the sushis, sashimis, noodles, tempuras, philadelphia rolls etc etc they have to offer. Or you can go "a la carte" and order from the menu. Note: it is customary for Japanese restaurants in Brazil to over fill your sake box, as a sign of generosity. Be sure to try the strawberry caipisake, to get the party started.

WHERE TO EAT: BENKEI
Rua Henrique Dumont 71, Ipanema tel: 2540-4829 or 2540-4830
Mon 7pm-12am; Tue-Sun 12pm-4pm & 7pm-12am
www.benkei.com.br

ARABIC

Ever been able to distinguish hummus from really good hummus? Or to bite a lamb steak sandwich and go "damn!"? At Amir, its all very apparent. They are just that good, with awards to back it. For those not too sure what to order to have a guaranteed amazing time: for openers: a combination, which includes hummus or babaganouch, labni, salad, esfiha, kibe and falafel, accompanied by pita bread. Main: *Shawarma* (lamb beef skewer with moroccan rice and *taboule* salad), with an optional side dish of crispy onions (not on the menu, but you can ask). After dinner: Arabic coffee, and puff a "narghile" (hookah). At lunch check out their all you can eat buffet till 4pm.

WHERE TO EAT: AMIR
Rua Ronald de Carvalho 55, Copacabana:: tel: 2275-5596
Rio Design Shopping Mall 3rd floor, Barra:: tel: 2431-1070
Both every day from 12pm to 12am. Copa Sun 6pm to 11pm

SPECIAL DEAL FOR OUR READERS CHECK BACK FLAP

ALL THE STUFF
YOU GOTTA TRY

GLOBO

GLOBO

DOCE
DE LEITE
EM PASTA

BRASIL

FOOD
STREET FOODS

PÃO DE QUEIJO:
Cheese puffs like you never had them before. Absolute must.

PASTEL DE CARNE:
Very much like a deep fried beef turn-over. Must try.

PASTEL DE QUEIJO/CAMARÃO:
Just like above, but with cheese or shrimp.

EMPADA DE CAMARÃO:
Shrimp cup pastry.

KIBE:
Arabic snack made from deep fried whole-wheat surrounding a spicy ground beef center.

COXINHA:
String chicken pastry inside deep-fried dough.

BOLINHO DE AIPIM:
Deep-fried cassava dough with a ground beef center.

CROQUETE DE CARNE:
Oven baked whole-wheat dough with ground beef center.

PÃO DE BATATA:
Potato bread with chicken, sausage, or ground beef center.

CACHORRO QUENTE (HOT DOG):
A variation of the NY style hotdog: bread, hot dog link, tomato paste with onions and peppers, then optionals: corn, string potatoes, parmesan and other stuff. Forget the other stuff.

CACHORRO QUENTE DE FORNO:
Oven baked hotdog in croissant shaped bread.

ESFIHA:
A tri-folded pizza of Arabic origin. Must have.

AND SNACKS

CHURROS:

Deep fried dough filled with none other than doce de leite (caramel's rich cousin). Then rolled in cinnamon sugar. Mmmmm good.

MISTO QUENTE:

Ham and cheese sandwich, made with stringy mozzarella. A must and usually very safe.

HAMBURGER/X-BURGER:

Hamburger/ Cheese-burger

X-TUDO:

Double cheese burger with everything they have to offer: bacon, fried egg, sausage, pulled chicken, string potatoes, etc etc.

SALSICHÃO:

A big hotdog link on a stick, grilled then pointlessly dipped in vinaigrette and *farofa*.

PASTEL DE FORNO:

Oven baked folded pie with various flavor fillings. Great usually.

BOLINHO DE BACALHAU:

Cod fish cake in ball format. Very good. Eat it with olive oil. Don't try the peppers.

FOLHEADO:

A flat croissant filed with ham and cheese, spinach or chicken

JOELHO:

The poor man's ham and cheese croissant. So doughy, you'll need 3 cokes to choke this down. Waste of money.

SANDUICHE NATURAL:

Simple sandwich lettuce, tomatoes, cheese and ham and or variations of these, without any condiments. Light and healthy.

BAR FOODS

PORÇÃO DE PASTEIS

Portion of the deep fried wontons, comes in different flavors (beef, cheese, shrimp or Cornish cheese) Where to try: Belmonte (Ipanema or Copa)

PORTION OF BOLINHO DE BACALHAU

Portion of cod fish cakes. Where to try: Bracarense (Leblon)

AIPIM FRITO

Deep fried cassava, a stringy cousin of the potato.

CARNE SECA COM AIPIM FRITO

Just like Aipim Frito but with sun dried jerked meat, very popular. Where to try: Informal (Leblon)

CALDO DE FEIJÃO

Bean soup with bacon bits.

FRANGO A PASSARINHO

Deep-fried chicken parts. All of them. Where to try: Sindicato do Chopp (Ipanema or Copa)

TORRESMO

Pork rinds, very macho (or nutritionally stupid). Where to try: Brasileirinho (Ipanema)

LINGUIÇA ACEBOLADA

Sausage and onions. Where to try: Barraca do Uruguai (Posto 9 Ipanema)

ISCA DE PEIXE

Deep fried and breaded tiny fish, somewhat disgusting, as you eat the entire fish: head, tails and all.

DESSERTS

If you are into desserts and all things sweet, you can't miss any of these, all of them Brazilian, all very, very sweet. (Sugar was so common in colonial Brazil that it was used in abundance).

BRIGADEIRO

Condensed milk meets chocolate on the stove, then is rolled into a ball and sprinkled with... chocolate sprinkles... must try.

PUDIM DE LEITE

Just like a "flan", but sweeter.

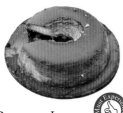

PUDIM DE CLARA

Before egg whites and sugar become a meringue, it becomes a *pudim de clara*, a very soft, sweet and airy pudding. A must for sweet-toothed people.

QUINDIM

Egg yolk and sugar and other sweet stuff makes this another must-try.

PASTEL DE BELÉM

Vanilla in an oven baked doughy cup. Portuguese dessert. Very good.

ROCAMBOLE

A roll with a *doce de leite* center... absolute must.

FRUIT SALAD

If you are on a diet, then a tropical fruit salad is in order.

BELEU

Crunchy bread nest with nuts and honey topping.

PUDIM DE CHOCOLATE

Not just a chocolate pudding, it is actually sweeter since its enhanced with condensed milk.

Stuff you

All these things can be found in the local supermarkets (Zona Sul, Sendas,

Doce de Leite

Caramel's cousin, but sweater, darker and creamier. Made from sugar and milk. Try it in bar and paste form

Geleia de Mocotó

Sweet bone-marrow jello, but definitely fun to eat. (Squeeze it between your teeth and cheek.)

(Reg. Trademark Arisco SA)

Danoninho

A thickened-up yogurt so small you must eat with the tiniest spoon available (borrow Barbie's).

(Reg. Trademark Danone LTDA)

Requeijão

Delicious creamy soft cheese easily spread over anything... anything!

(Reg. Trademark -Santa Clara LTDA)

Torrone

A chewy bar with peanuts or cashew nuts. Italian origin, but now nationalized in Brazil.

Bombom Garoto

A box with an assortment of different bonbons and miniature chocolate bars. Great to have at the hotel.

(Reg. Trademark- Chocolate Garoto S.A)

NEVER ATE

Pão de Açucar etc). They all make great gifts for your friends and family.

PALMITO- HEART OF PALM

The center of a Palm tree's trunk. Buy a jar and eat them straight. If you don't like it, send it to me.

COCADA

Coconut slivers mixed with thick sugary paste. Very, very sweet.

AMENDOIM JAPONÊS

Japanese peanuts. Peanuts with a crunchy shell. Great to have around at all times.

(Reg. Trademark AGTAL A. Guedes Torrefação de Amendoim LTDA)

BISCOITO

Cookies.

(Reg. Trademark Bauducco & Cia LTDA)

BISCOITO DE POLVILHO

The best alternative to potato chips. Oven baked fluffy manioc flour biscuit. Great at the beach (ask for *biscoito Globo*, or wave to the guy with a big plastic bag).

(Reg. Trademark Pan. Mandarino LTDA)

PAÇOQUINHA

Peanut powder compressed into a bar. Very good.

PÉ DE MOLEQUE

Peanut brittle. Roasted peanuts joined by hardened molasses.

EVERYTHING YOU

Alcoholic
(Let's talk about these first)

CERVEJA

From an international point of view, all Brazilian beers taste the same: they are all lagers or pilsners, as any other type of beer would not agree with the weather. Given an option, ask for Devassa, Skol or Cerpa.

CHOPP

A light draft beer on tap. Preferred over bottled beer. Ask for Devassa or Brahma.

CAIPIRINHA

The most refreshing alcoholic mixed-drink in the world! Cachaça, lime, sugar and ice. Great on any occasion: bar, restaurant, clubbing, breakfast. Just don't buy it from street vendors, as they sometimes use ice made from unfiltered water that can make you sick. Also, try the caipivodka (with vodka) and the caipisake (with sake, duh). And some trendier bars offer it with different fruits: pineapple, strawberry, tangerine etc. When given a choice of cachaça, opt for the ones from the north of Minas Gerais or from Salinas.

BATIDA DE CÔCO

Very creamy drink, will get you drunk without you knowing it. Coconut milk, rum, sugar and other stuff blended into a milkshake.

A SHOT OF PINGA

Cachaça (pr: ca-sha-ssa)

Only for the macho. Straight cowboy shot of pinga. You won't need to display your ignorance further.

PINGA COM MEL

Cachaça with honey, mixed to a point where you don't taste the cachaça at all. You can drink it all night and wake up sober. Now that's responsible boozing.

CHILEAN WINES

Brazilian wines haven't quite made it yet. While down here, go for the affordable Santa Carolina, or the full bodied Casileiro Del Diablo from Concha&Toro.

SHOULD DRINK
Non Alcoholic

COFFEE

Since the weather is hot, you don't want to walk around with a steaming pint of coffee, so people drink shot-sized cups of very concentrated coffee, to get the kick without raising your body temp.

AGUA DE COCO

Coconut water, not milk. Very good for whenever you are dehydrating. Two will cure most hangovers.

GUARANÁ

The most popular Brazilian soft drink, great on any occasion.

(Reg. Trademark AmBev SA LTDA)

MATE

A strong-flavored iced tea from the south of Brazil, made from the mate herb. Available in diet or regular and in natural or lemon flavored.

(Reg. Trademark Leão LTDA)

AGUA

Since tap water is not drinkable in Brazil, you should always look for bottled water. SEM gas= non-carbonated, COM gas= carbonated.

(Reg. Trademark Alimentos e Bebidas Campos do Jordão LTDA)

ADES JUICES

Tasty soy milk juices made from various fruits, found in super-markets.

(Reg. Trademark Unilever Best Foods Brasil LTDA)

FRUITS AND JUICES

The fastest way to try all the various fruits is to hit a fruit market and walk around buying one of each.
Otherwise, any of the juice bars have these and others in juice form.

MANGA –MANGO

Considered
by many the
one fruit they
would take
with them
to a desert
island. Sweet
and creamy.
Vitamin A and C.

GOIABA- GUAVA

Thick,
sweet and
smooth,
just like
me.
Vitamin A,
C,complex
B and other

minerals. Not recommended for
those with digestive problems.

MAMÃO - PAPAYA

Just as healthy
as avocado,
papaya milk
shake is great
for your
intestinal
works. Vitamin
A and C, a
natural laxative
and stress reliever.

MARACUJÁ- PASSION FRUIT

Slightly bitter to a point that it
makes your cheeks pucker. but
great as a

refreshment. Rich in complex
B vitamins, iron and has natural
soothing properties.

CAJÚ- CASHEW

Sweet and
refreshing
with a very
distinguished
taste and smell.
Rich in vitamin
A, C and
complex B.

CANA- SUGAR CANE

The
sweetest of
all things
on God's
green earth.
Always
squeezed on
the spot for best flavor.

ABACATE - AVOCADO

Thick and creamy, avocado milk
shake. It has
the largest
number of
nutrients and
vitamins.
Great for
breakfast.

ACEROLA

The
king of
vitamin
C (each
has more
Vim.
C than
40 lemons), acerola juice is
refreshing and slightly citric.

ACAÍ

Blended
together with
guarana, acai
shakes (or
very thick
smoothies)
should be
consumed with a spoon, and
optionally a side of granola
for sprinkling. Very caloric yet
rich in proteins, fiber, vitamin
E, minerals and a natural
cholesterol controller.

Fruit fair weekly schedule:
Remember: They all end at 1pm!
Mon: Rua Henrique Dumont (Ipanema)
Tues: Praça General Osorio (Ipanema)

Wed: Praça Edmundo Bittencourt (Copa)
Thu: Rua Min. Viveiro de Castro (Copa)
Fri: Praça N. S. Paz (Ipanema)

Sat: Rua Frei Leandro (Jardin Botanico)
Sun: Rua Serzedelo Correia (Copa)

COCO - COCONUT WATER

The best thing when you are dehydrating under the sun. Drink 2 to cure your hangover. Rich in minerals, potassium, and sodium.

GUARANÁ

Sold normally in refreshment form (refresco), guaraná could be considered a distant cousin of the root beer, but, just like every juice in Brazil, a lot sweeter. A stimulant and digestion facilitator. And dig this: clinically proven to enhance sexual performance.

PITANGA

Healthy fruit with citrony yet milky taste. Rich in calcium, iron and phosphorus. A natural stimulant and anti-diarrhea.

FRUTA DO CONDE

Aka Custard AppleUgly on the outside (looks like a grenade), sweet on the inside. Talk about philosophical dualities! Very milky juice. Vitamin C and complex B.

JABUTICABA

A distant cousin of the grape, yet sweeter and thicker. Great in fruit form, specially when frozen. Bite, spit the seed and skin out. Rich in complex B vitamins.

AMORA

Dark latin raspberry. A highly effective cholesterol reducer.

CARAMBOLA

Star shaped football with a juicy and citrony zing to it. Great in fruit or juice form.

MATE

Slightly caffeined herb used to make iced tea with a deep rich flavor.

CAMÚ-CAMÚ

Great name, but that's it. Terrible dirt-like taste. Good for practical jokes.

WHAT'S THE

POOR PEOPLE IN RICH AREAS?

They come to nicer neighborhoods to beg from the rich (makes sense), but donation is not recommended unless they have a condition. Many of the beggars in working condition choose to beg. Don't give them anything, as this doesn't help anybody. If you want to help, check page 72 on how to give back.

FLANELINHAS?

These are shines that watch your car for a few R$. You pay them R$2 and they don't kick your rear view mirror off; fair and square. Each owns a block, and is responsible for whatever happens to your car. Since that is where they will permanently work for a few years, should something go missing, you can find them the next day, and open a can of whoop-ass.

STREET VENDORS EVERYWHERE?

Selling mostly stuff made in China, street vendors account for about 1/3 of Brazil's work force. This type of business is illegal but frequently overlooked, as most escape the regulating street cops.

BEACH VENDORS?

Just like the street vendors, the beach vendors tend to offer more practical stuff like snacks, ice cream, beer or sunglasses. Forget the hammock guy.

DOG TV?

These are rotisserie chicken ovens, referred to as television for dogs. For around R$8 you can get diced chicken to go.

RECKLESS DRIVING?

Since most Brazilians bought their license, or forgot most of the rules and regulations, everyone drives like its Super Nintendo. Interestingly, every year there is one traffic law which is fashionable to follow. This year it is to not stop at pedestrian crossing stripes. All other rules are ignored.

BLOWING STOPLIGHTS AT NIGHT?

For safety reasons, most people slow down at red lights, check for traffic, then speed up again, as stopping at a red light in the dark can be dangerous, due to car robbing.

DEAL WITH...?

LACK OF TRIBES?

Where are the punks? The nerds? The hippies? The heroin addicts? The grungy? The reggae? Rio doesn't have visible amount of any of the above. It is mostly preppies, jiu-jitsu fighters (pit bulls), artsy-fartsy (neo-hippies) and normal people. You can find all these tribes in São Paulo.

SHANTY TOWNS ON THE HILLS EVERYWHERE?

Why do the poor have the views, while the rich are locked down to the flat areas? A law from when Brazil was still a colony is still in use, which prohibits anyone from building on the hill sides, to allow Cariocas to have a green view from wherever they live. In the last 40 years, the hills have been overtaken by the poor, and the government has had little luck stopping them.

EXCESSIVE WAITERS?

Given that the minimum wage is R$380 (US$190 per month), most businesses can afford a large staff to improve service. Unfortunately, most of this staff is under-trained, which lowers the quality of service.

WHAT RACE ARE BRAZILIANS?

Brazilians are a mixture of different ethnic groups, so mixed for so long you commonly get 16 shades of white to black to Indian to Asian. Sociologists consider this mixture a meta-race, since a true genetic melting pot is still at work, decanting weak genes and physical traits.

HOT WOMEN BY THE SIDE OF THE ROAD?

The tall, hot prostitutes are state-of-the-art transvestites or transsexuals. Don't fall in love.

YOUNG PEOPLE HANGING OUT IN GAS STATIONS?

Gas stations have become a gathering place for different groups to hang around, blast music and sip beer, probably because they are one of the few convenience stores open at night.

THE LACK OF BMWS AND LUXURY CARS?

Brazilians get hit with 100% tariff on imported cars, so a BMW325e goes for about US$60K. And given that most wealthy Brazilians don't want to make themselves a visible target for car-jackers, most members of the upper class prefer regular cars.

WHAT'S THE DEAL WITH CONSUMING BEER ANYWHERE?

I know, isn't it great?

DOING BUSINESS

If you can't stop thinking of business ideas even when on vacation, you may want to check out some of these sites and take these guidelines into consideration.

2006 STATS

Population: 187 million

GDP: $673 billion (+5.2% from 2005)

GDP (per sector): Agriculture: 10.1%, Industry, 38.6%, Services: 51.3%

Inflation rate: 7.6%

Unemployment rate: 11.5%

Exports: $100 billion

Imports $61 billion

GUIDELINES

1 Smile: When meeting someone for the first time for a presentation, or talking to secretaries on the telephone to arrange appointments, Brazilians will engage with you much more easily if you appear happy and enthusiastic. Too much seriousness will not usually help your progress.

2 Patience: In Brazil things generally take longer to get accomplished. Even though many Brazilians have international experience in Europe and the US, very often they do not have the same sense of urgency you will be used to. When setting time frames and deadlines for decisions, be sure to build in lots of additional flexibility.

3 Meet people: sure, Brazilian businessmen love their Blackberries and Palm-pilot PDAs as much as anyone else, however face-to-face communication is 100 times more effective here. Brazilians

are big on building trust through personal contacts.

4 Don't assume all Brazilians have the same work ethic. Brazil is larger than Europe and each of the 27 states will demand a slightly different approach. As a general rule, the southern states of Rio Grande do Sul, Paraná, Santa Caterina and Sao Paulo operate on similar standards to the USA and Europe. The Carioca businessperson from Rio de Janeiro is an entirely different negotiator. A positive assessment would say he is a very friendly, warm, creative, witty entrepreneur with a large imagination, almost theatrical ability in verbal communication with a highly developed intuitive vision for making money. A negative assessment would state that punctuality and calling you back is not their strength. Given these two assessments, the main piece of advice is BE PATIENT!

5 Never, ever, try to bullshit a Brazilian when doing business, particularly the Carioca. First of all, it will not work. Any attempt to pull one over on your potential partner/customer will not only backfire but will also prevent any future dealings with this person and likely anyone he knows.

6 Bureaucracy: One of the most frustrating aspects of doing business in Brazil. Be

prepared to wait in line for long periods of time at government and administrative offices, banks and other services. Bring a book to read.

7 Mobile phones: do not bother trying to get a post-paid subscription if you are not based permanently in Brazil. Simply buy a pre-paid chip at one of the many mobile operators: TIM, OI and Claro are the most popular. You can rent one (check next page)

8 Bank accounts: you will not be able to open a bank account unless you have a valid passport, a CPF and a 12-month residence permit. The CPF and residence permit must be applied for at the Policia Federal and can take months to be processed.

9 Learn some basic Portuguese: it may seem obvious, but even if you make a lot of mistakes, your efforts will be greatly appreciated and progress will be quicker. Look for our language CD "Portuguese For Tourists", available at www.portuguese-crash-course.com

10 Trust is extremely important when closing a deal; be prepared to conduct several meetings before a final decision is made. Also, always go for the top decision-makers: Brazil is big on the hierarchical structures and if the top guy wants something he will override all others.

IN BRAZIL

WEBSITES

For general information:
www.brazilinfocenter.org

For a more detailed look on how to conduct yourself during business meetings:
www.executiveplanet.com/business-eti-quette/Brazil.html

For general information on investment issues:
www.latinfocus.com/latinfocus/factsheets/brazil/brafact_econ_investment.htm

For a list of vendors and business opportunities:
www.brazilbiz.com.br/english/

Online News sites:
www.investnews.net (Eng + Pt)
www.brazzil.com (Eng)
www.infobrazil.com (Eng)

Other useful links

Government of Brazil
www.brazil.gov.br

BUSINESS TRAVEL

Brazil's number one leisure tourism destination, Rio is also the most popular business tourism location in Latin America. Riocentro is considered the best and largest convention center in the continent. If you are looking to organize any incentive trips to motivate employees, Rio is the place. For more information on organizing such trips, check out this link:
www.rioconventionbureau.com.br

For a more detailed look at doing business in Rio and the rest of Brazil, it is a good idea to check out the relevant chamber of commerce sites:
www.britcham.com.br (UK)
www.amchamrio.com.br (US)
www.ahkbrasil.com (Germany)
www.italcam.com.br (Italy)

Other sites to consult include:
www.brazilchamber.org/resources/do-ing_br.htm (Brazilian American Chamber of Commerce)
www.bndes.gov.br (Brazilian Social and Economic Development Bank)
www.desenvolvimento.gov.br (Ministry of Industry and Commerce)
www.mre.gov.br (Ministry of Foreign Affairs)

If you are thinking of quitting your job, selling everything and investing in Brazil, check out this site:
www.braziltradenet.gov.br

And for some of the pitfalls and difficulties of doing business in brazil:
www.brazilbrazil.com

CHAUFFEUR SERVICE
Marcelo Esteves (UK,ES)
9984-7654 or marafes@terra.com.br

TRANSLATION SERVICES
Steve Yolen
yolen@amcham.com.br
9612-4938

PORTUGUESE LESSONS
Dynamic Portuguese School
Contact: Jose Hordones tel: 9961-6847
dynamic.rlk@terra.com.br

Moving to Brazil

Many foreigners have moved to Rio: half to work, half to retire. The attraction is, as Dan Babush puts it, "As soon as you arrive you are instantly 3 times richer, 3 inches taller and 3 times more relaxed than back home".

Rio is ideal for those who can web-commute: its time zone is 1 to 4 hours ahead of the US, allowing you to wake up late. Those who come looking for work end up teaching English, as the job market is tight and underpaid.

What many foreigners end up doing is spending 6 months at home, getting paid and saving, then coming to Rio, and living it up for 6 months.

To get an idea: rent in Ipanema/Leblon goes for at least R$3000 (2bdr), groceries, cellular phone, transport (taxi) and maid another R$1200. Then nightlife, getaways, shopping and flights back home are up to you.

If you are considering moving to Rio and want to learn more, or need help with finding a place, the paperwork or legal assistance, contact:
Standard Imóveis Ltda
Rua Visconde de Pirajá 414 / 1214
Quartier Ipanema
22410-002 or 2267-5016 or 2247-9511
standard@standardimoveis.com.br
www.standardimoveis.com.br

GREAT DESTINATIONS CLOSE TO RIO

There are two ways to extend your vacation in Brazil. One way is to visit the neighboring tourist spots in the state of Rio; the other is to take a plane or bus to other popular tourist destinations. If you intend on coming back on future trips to different parts of Brazil, we highly recommend staying in the state of Rio. It offers a little of everything Brazil is known for, namely parties, beaches, jungle and colonial history. All these spots take under 3 hours to get to, by bus or car.

If you are staying longer than 7 days in Rio, we highly recommend checking out these neighboring areas, as they each offer things that Rio doesn't: Búzios is a party town with great beaches, the Petropolis area is great for mountainous sports, Ilha Grande has the best eco-tourism of the state, and Paraty is knee-deep in culture, history and cuteness.

Paraty 👍👍👍👍
Historic town with beautiful beaches

Ilha Grande 👍👍👍👍
Eco-tourism heaven

SITES TO CHECK OUT:

www.brazilmax.com
www.buziosonline.com
www.braziltour.com
www.justbrazil.org
www.v-brazil.com
www.brazilink.org
www.amazonbrasil.com.br
www.brazil-travel-guide.com
www.braziltravelinformation.com
www.braziltravelvacation.com

Buzios 👍👍👍👍

The party town of the Southern Hemisphere

Petropolis & Itaipava 👍👍👍

Imperial city in cozy mountain range

Rio de Janeiro

100 KM

100 MILES

Rio For Partiers

BÚZIOS

Must Experience

Búzios is the St. Tropez of South America, without the snobbery. Between December and March you can find the trendy 30 somethings, as well as the young crowd, mostly partiers and surfers.

It has a complete tourist infrastructure that lets you stay a week without getting bored. It is a claw shaped peninsula, with about 27 beaches.

Reservations are recommended for the week around X-mas, New Year and Carnival. Otherwise, finding a place to stay won't be hard, as it accommodates thousands of people during high season. Look for a pousada at Geribá (the coolest beach and where you will be spending your daytime) or downtown close to "Rua das Pedras" (Centro) where you will be spending your nighttime. Other areas will be out of the way and not worth the savings.

To get to Búzios, take the 1001 bus from the Novo Rio Bus Station, which takes 3 hours. Or you can hire a car service for speed and comfort. Once there, you can rent a dune buggy or a car. Other good dates to go are during national holidays, should they land on a weekday, as everyone in Rio uses a sick day and makes it a 4-day weekend. Check: www.buziosonline.com.br

ACTIVITIES:

Surf lessons and body board rentals (Geribá), wind surfing (Manguinhos), wake boarding (Ferradura Beach), jet skiing (Centro Beach)

NIGHTTIME:

Different clubs and bars along Rua das Pedras.

QUICK DECISION MAKER:

Main activities: Partying, dancing, beach, eating, surfing, windsurfing, jetskiing, snorkelling, etc.

Who usually goes: Singles, couples, groups

When to go: All year round on weekends, all week December to March. How long to stay: 3 to 10 days.

Who can organize your trip:

Rio Charm
Contact: Bryan at info@riocharm.com :: www.riocharm.com
Rio 8606-7497 or US 1-305 767-4525
Packages to Buzios start at R$290 pp for 3 nights including transfer, elegant *pousada* (inn) and schooner tour.

BUZIOS?
THAT'S ALSO
WITH TIM.
THE LARGEST GSM
COVERAGE IN BRAZIL.
TIM
Viver sem fronteiras

NIGHTLIFE

Centro

Ferradura

Geriba

DAYTIME

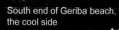

South end of Geriba beach, the cool side

Two in the morning outside Guapo Loco, on Rua das Pedras

ILHA GRANDE

Must Experience

Ilha Grande used to be where they incarcerated Brazil's most violent criminals, until they deactivated the prison and now it is a wildlife preserve, so much so, no cars are allowed, only walking and sailing around it. Given its size (hence the name Big Island) you should stay at a strategic place like Vila do Abraão, where there are plenty of affordable *pousadas*, restaurants and relaxed nightlife. Don't expect big parties, but live music shows and luaus. Don't go during New Year or Carnival, as it gets packed and unbearable. More at: www. ilhagrande.com.br

ILHA GRANDE?
THAT'S ALSO
WITH TIM.

THE LARGEST GSM
COVERAGE IN BRAZIL

TIM
Viver sem fronteiras

ACTIVITIES

The island offers a lot: diving, surfing, hiking, cycling, rappeling and trekking, as well as eco-tours and tours of the various forts and prisons.

QUICK DECISION MAKER

Main activities: Partying, dancing, singing, beach, eating, sailing, drinking etc.

Who usually goes: Singles, couples, groups

When to go: All year round.

How long to stay: 4 to 10 days

Who can organize your trip:

Gray Line Tours
Contact: Sales
2512-9919 reservas@grayline.com.br
www.grayline.com.br
Grayline has single day tours to Ilha Grande at afford-able prices. Tours leave early and return late, and need 24hr booking.

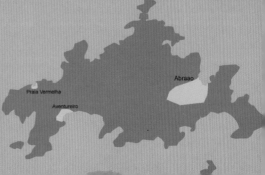

Abraao

Praia Vermelha

Aventureiro

ANGRA

Angra, on the other hand, is where Brazil's millionaires hang during the summer, usually on their private islands. Since Angra's coast is extremely rugged, there are tons of beautiful bays, and the water clear. You can stay at one of the few resorts there, or rent a villa and bring all your friends. Considering that the tiki hut restaurants, snorkeling and hiking are on islands, boating is a necessity for island hopping.

ANGRA ALSO HAS TIM.

THE LARGEST GSM COVERAGE IN BRAZIL.

TIM
Viver sem fronteiras

PETRÓPOLIS & ITAIPAVA

Petrópolis and Itaipava are excellent options when the forecast predicts cloudy weather for the next few days. These neighboring towns work off each other: whatever one doesn't have, the other does. And since they are all very close, you should rent a car in Rio, drive up the mountain range (which in itself is a fun drive with endless scary-but-safe curves) and stay at one of the bungalows in Itaipava.

Most of the young bars, clubs and lounges are in Itaipava, while the daytime activities are spread between the 2 cities: rappel, rafting, zip line, canyoning, cycling, trekking, horseback riding, dirt road motor biking etc. For a cultural experience, visit the Imperial Palace in Petrópolis. These 2 cities can be toured in under 3 days.

QUICK DECISION MAKER

Main activities: Trekking, rappeling, climbing, rafting, museums, fine eating.

Who usually goes: Couples, groups

When to go: All year round, specially June to August

How long to stay: 2 to 5 days

Who can organize your trip:
Rio Charm
Contact: Bryan
info@riocharm.com :: www.riocharm.com
Rio 8606-7497 or US 1-305 767-4525
Packages to Itaipava start at R$360 pp for 3 nights including transfer, elegant _pousada_ (inn) and historic tour.

TIM IN PETRÓPOLIS, IN ITAIPAVA, AND IN THE WHOLE BRAZIL.

THE ONLY OPERATOR WITH GSM COVERAGE ALL OVER BRAZIL.

TIM
Viver sem fronteiras

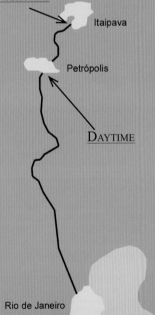

NIGHTLIFE

Itaipava

Petrópolis

DAYTIME

Rio de Janeiro

Paraty

Trindade

PARATY

One of the cutest and most historic cities along Brazil's coast. Founded in the 16th Century, it still has colonial architecture in the downtown area. Not the best place if you are single, but definitely a great option for couples or mixed groups of friends. Stay at one of the *pousadas* on the beaches just east of downtown, where the rates are very affordable (R$75/double) while still close to the action.

There are great dining options in Paraty, all found in the historic center. For night life, you are limited to a few live music bars. But you could also have a luau for you and your friends at any of the beaches, since Paraty is pretty safe.

Day time activities include: rafting, rappel, schooner trip, surfing, fishing, off-road cycling, etc.

For cultural, do the "Gold Trail" tour, which takes you along part of the road where gold was transported in colonial times. Then go to Fazenda Moycana, a sugar cane farm from 200 years ago, it is well preserved, with water falls, free-range peacocks and hearty Brazilian food.

More at: www.paraty.com.br

QUICK DECISION MAKER

Main activities: Beach, trekking, eating, sailing, drinking etc.

Who usually goes: couples

When to go: All year round.

How long to stay: 2 to 5 days

Who can organize your trip:
Rio Charm
Contact: Bryan
info@riocharm.com :: www.riocharm.com
Rio 8606-7497 or US 1-305 767-4525
Packages to Paraty start at R$340 pp for 3 nights including transfer, elegant *pousada* (inn) and schooner tour.

PARATY ALSO HAS TIM.

THE LARGEST GSM COVERAGE IN BRAZIL.

TIM
Viver sem fronteiras

The streets are below sea-level, so the tide washes the city.

The centuries old downtown area is safe to explore at night.

Luxury & Honeymoon

We have layed out two honeymoon/luxury getaway plans: the more affordable "Around Rio" trip and the more diverse "Around Brazil" plan.

Brazil's romantic spots can go toe to toe with most honeymoon getaways found in the rest of the world: its beauty is on par with the best, its excitement is real and not "plastic" and prices are extremely affordable.

Rio For Partiers

AROUND RIO

Quick breakdown: 3 days in Buzios, 3 in Rio, 3 in Angra.

After landing in Rio, dart over to Buzios, opting for a dreamlike resort such as Casas Brancas. There you can visit the 27 beaches during the day, speed around in a boat and fine dine and sip some bubbly the night away.

Then hop over to Rio, which, as you have been reading, is just amazing, and 3 days are a

must. You can stay in a 5 star hotel like Caesar Park and visit the popular attractions, while dancing to samba and bossa nova after dinner.

Then swing over to Angra, and lodge in the Pestana beach

Trip Ideas

What's cool about these resorts is that they can offer a true "get away from the problems of the world" type holiday, given their seclusion from big cities.

The most positive feedback from honeymooners is when they experience the exotic beaches of the northeast for 4-5 days, such as the Txai in Itacare, the Nannai in Porto de Galinhas or Pousada Maravilha on the island of Fernando de Noronha, mix it up by heading down to Rio for 2-3 days and finish with 3 days either sailing in Angra or dancing the night away in upbeat sophisticated Buzios.

bungalow. There you can visit any of the 365 islands, snorkel or dive, or sit at the beach waiting for the sunset.

From researching a few travel agencies, this package usually starts around US$5500 for two people.

AROUND BRAZIL

Conversely, if you have more money to spend and want to explore more of Brazil, you can jet around for 11 days to Brazil's top resorts. And here is a little list with the top 10 I found very useful (however, it is my opinion that all these are number one).

Top Ten Honeymoon Resorts

1.Txai, Itacare

2.Nannai, Porto de Galinhas

3.Maravilha, Fernando de Noronha

4.Ponto Dos Ganchos, Floripa

5.Casas Brancas, Buzios

6.Estrela D'Agua, Trancoso

7.Pestana, Angra Dos Reis

8.Copacabana Palace. Rio

9. Sitio do Lobo, Angra dos Reis

10.Etnia, Trancoso

If couples are interested in experiencing culture then you can swap Rio for Salvador to immerse them in the Black Heart of Brazil, a truly tantalizing experience for all five senses.

BRAZIL AT A GLANCE

If you plan visiting other parts of Brazil, your first stop should be Salvador, which overflows with Afro-Brazilian culture, music, costumes, food and mellowness. Another option during the summer is to hop over to Natal, then to Pipa and its neighboring towns. This is surfer&babes paradise. Fernando de Noronha has some of the most beautiful beaches in the world, as well as an incredibly well kept sea life; ideal for divers. Porto Seguro is among the best party towns in the southern hemisphere. If you want to see jungle, people have been having fuller experiences in the Pantanal than the Amazon. You get closer to the animals, you see more and you have more activities to partake in.

Fortaleza ♨♨   Beach & Party

Manaus ♨♨♨ Amazon Ecotourism

Beach & scuba heaven♨♨♨♨ Fernando de Noronha

Dunes Ecotourism ♨♨♨ João Pessoa

Recife ♨♨♨ Culture & Beach

Salvador ♨♨♨♨ Culture & Party

Porto Seguro ♨♨♨♨ Party Town

Brasilia ♨♨ Architecture

Bonito ♨♨♨ Ecotourism

Ouro Preto ♨♨♨ Culture & Party

Rio de Janeiro ♨♨♨♨

São Paulo ♨♨ Business & Party

Foz do Iguacu ♨♨♨ Waterfalls

Florianopolis ♨♨♨♨ Beach & Party Town

Porto Alegre ♨♨   Party Town

SALVADOR

If Rio is Brazil's face, Salvador is Brazil's heart. You arrive and you notice something in the air that makes you want to move to a new rhythm. Salvador is probably the most culture rich city in Brazil, offering a spectrum of music, food, dance, art and architecture. Everyone seems willing to leave work and party if someone starts playing a little guitar a block away. Lot's of foreigners arrived and could never leave, opening bed and breakfasts as their reason to stay. Salvador maintains its roots while embracing what works.

Salvador deserves at least 7 days, as it is surrounded by enchanting places like Morro de Sao Paulo, a party island 2 hours south, Praia do Forte, a fisherman village turned beach get-away one hour north and Cachoeira, a historic town one hour west.

To skip Salvador is to miss a place where your heart beats faster.

If you enjoyed this guide, look for Salvador For Partiers (www.salvadorforpartiers. com). Or check www.bahia-online.net

QUICK DECISION MAKER

Main activities: Partying, dancing, singing, beach, eating, sailing, drinking etc.

Who usually goes: Singles, couples, groups

When to go: Year round.

How long to stay: 4 to 10 days.

Who can organize your trip:

Rio Charm
Contact: Bryan
info@riocharm.com :: www.riocharm.com
Rio 8606-7497 or US 1-305 767-4525
Packages to Salvador start at R$1100 pp for 3 nights including air tickets, transfer, elegant pousada (inn) and city tour.

Bahia

Praia do Forte
Salvador
Morro de Sao Paulo

SALVADOR?
THAT'S ALSO
WITH TIM.

THE LARGEST GSM
COVERAGE IN BRAZIL.

TIM
Viver sem fronteiras

Rio For Parties

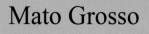

Mato Grosso

Cuiabá

Pantanal

THE PANTANAL
AND THE WHOLE
BRAZIL HAVE TIM.

THE ONLY OPERATOR
WITH GSM COVERAGE
ALL OVER BRAZIL.

TIM
Viver sem fronteiras

PANTANAL

The Pantanal, portuguese for swamp-lands, is an amazing part of Brazil most of the world has never heard of. Sure, the Amazon is great, but most who visit both prefer the Pantanal. Why? You get closer to Brazilian animals, such as ant-eaters, capivaras, large birds and various fresh-water fish. This is not a party destination, but a beer is a finger-lift away from your fishing rod on your boat. At night, bonfire warmed up by caipirinhas or, heck, straight *cachaça*, so macho you'll grow extra hair on your chest. If available, opt for the 3 day river boat trip, where you get to live a real African Queen experience.

QUICK DECISION MAKER

Main activities: Crystal-blue river scuba diving, jungle exploring, animal photo-hunting (you get that close), fishing and trekking

Who usually goes: Couples, groups

When to go: April to November weekdays.

How long to stay: 3 to 8 days

Who can organize your trip:
Rio Charm
Contact: Bryan
info@riocharm.com :: www.riocharm.com
Rio 8606-7497 or US 1-305 767-4525
Packages to Bonito start at R$2000 pp for 3 nights including air tickets, transfer, elegant pousada (inn) and river tour.

Rio For Partiers

NATAL

Mix year-round warm weather, crystal clear coral reefs, sand dunes, beaches, history and an active nightlife and you get Natal, on the northeast corner of Brazil. Two hours south are Pipa and Ponta Negra, two charming beach villages preferred by young Scandinavians and Brazilians alike. Zen atmosphere during the day with naturesque bars and restaurants at night.

More at: www.natal-brazil.com

QUICK DECISION MAKER

Main activities: Sand-dune buggying, beach chilling, chilling in Pipa (2 hours south), scuba diving and sea fishing.

Who usually goes: Groups, partiers

When to go: Year-round, weekends.

How long to stay: 4 to 7 days

Who can organize your trip:
Rio Charm
Contact: Bryan
info@riocharm.com :: www.riocharm.com
Rio 8606-7497 or US 1-305 767-4525
Packages to Natal start at R$1400 pp for 3 nights including air tickets, transfer, elegant pousada (inn) and dune tour.

NATAL?
THAT'S ALSO
WITH TIM.

THE LARGEST GSM
COVERAGE IN BRAZIL.

TIM
Viver sem fronteiras

RIO GRANDE
DO NORTE

Natal

Rio For Partiers

Manaus

AMAZONAS

TIM IN RIO, IN THE
AMAZON, AND IN
THE WHOLE BRAZIL.

**THE ONLY OPERATOR
WITH GSM COVERAGE
ALL OVER BRAZIL.**

TIM

Viver sem fronteiras

AMAZON

At the heart of the Amazon rain-forest lies the city of Manaus, located at the junction of the two main arteries that form the Amazon river. The Amazon is one of those places that makes humans seem small; huge trees and rivers so wide you can't see the other bank.

As for main activities, you can do a little jungle exploring and photo-hunting, tree-top cabling or riverboat fishing.

QUICK DECISION MAKER

Main activities: Jungle exploring

Who usually goes: Groups, couples

When to go: Year round, weekdays.

How long to stay: 3 to 5 days

Who can organize your trip:
Rio Charm
Contact: Bryan
info@riocharm.com :: www.riocharm.com
Rio 8606-7497 or US 1-305 767-4525
Packages to Manaus start at R$1800 pp
for 3 nights including air tickets, transfer,
elegant pousada (inn) and river tour.

FOZ DO IGUASSU

One of the world's most impressive developments of nature is the Iguassu Falls, a series of 300ft waterfalls 20 miles wide.

The town itself serves the tourists, with lots of finessed restaurants, bars and clubs. The average stay is 3 days, which is enough to see the main attractions: several falls, the power dam, rafting and rapid-canoeing (not down the main falls, of course) and a jungle tour.

QUICK DECISION MAKER

Main activities: Waterfall sightseeing, trekking, rafting and canoeing

Who usually goes: Couples

When to go: Year round, weekdays.

How long to stay: 2 to 4 days

Who can organize your trip:
Rio Charm
Contact: Bryan
info@riocharm.com :: www.riocharm.com
Rio 8606-7497 or US 1-305 767-4525

Packages to Foz do Iguassu start at R$1100 pp for 3 nights including air tickets, transfer, elegant pousada (inn) and river tour.

PARANÁ

Foz do Iguassu

FOZ DO IGUASSU AND THE WHOLE BRAZIL HAVE TIM.

THE ONLY OPERATOR WITH GSM COVERAGE ALL OVER BRAZIL.

TIM
Viver sem fronteiras

How to Pay Less Than Locals

Just use the RFP Disocunt Coupons with any of our partnered establishments. Tear the coupon off, give it to the manager/instructor and ask for the discount.

We have partnered with many of the establishments and services found in this book (they have a [SPECIAL DEAL FOR OUR READERS / CHECK BACK FLAP] next to their info). They have agreed to honor a bonus or discount in accordance with what is stated in the coupons in the back flap. **All discounts and bonuses valid through June 2008.**

Hotels, restaurants, bars and clubs want to maintain a clean image and **may not honor their discount commitments to tourists accompanied by ladies of the night.**

PLEASE CHECK FOR THE LATEST PARTNER UPDATES

While we strongly believe that they will all comply with the terms of partnership, some may (at their discretion) stop offering discounts or bonuses. Please check our website for the latest updates, so you don't spend time on places and activities without freebies. Just visit www.rioforpartiers.com and click on the UPDATES section.

IN CASE OF POOR OR UNFAIR TREATMENT

We have done our homework so that you may have a great experience in Rio. The hand-picked establishments named in this book are known for their quality of service. Should you be poorly or unfairly treated by any of these establishments, please let us know so we may consider removing them from future publications. Email us any complaints at support@rioforpartiers.com

PRICES

All prices are in Reals (R$) unless preceded by US$. At the time of publication the exchange rate is R$1.9 to US$1. All prices are subject to change without notice (but do check the UPDATES link on our website www.rioforpartiers.com)

ONE-TIME USE

One discount per person per coupon. If you have a group of people travelling with you, get each person a copy of this book, so I sell more books and you can all save tons while in Rio. We all win.

HOW TO SCHEDULE A TOUR OR LESSON:

All the guides and sports instructors listed here speak fluent English, so your job is to only make the phone call and schedule a pick-up time. If you do ask for a hotel (or hostel) concierge to schedule a day tour for you, the discount will not apply and you may end up paying the regular rate.

To call, you can either use the telephone in your room or hostel, or use a calling card at the nearest phone booth.

PHONE BOOTH INSTRUCTIONS:

To use a regular phone booth, remove the receiver, insert your calling card and dial the number. Once you are done talking, you may hang up and remove your card. You do not need to dial 21 when dialing from inside Rio.

Want to write a For Partiers guide to your city? Email cris@rioforpartiers.com or visit www.forpartiers.com